"If you're looking to plan a wedding that feels like yours and not your grand-mother's, then you need this book. With warmth and humor, Christopher Shelley uses his years of experience as a celebrant to lay out everything you need to make your ceremony fun and memorable for everyone. Don't worry, Grandma will love it, too."

> —Jennifer Wright, author of *It Ended Badly: 13 of the Worst Break-Ups in History* (happily married to Daniel Kibblesmith)

"Christopher Shelley tells it all with the panache, wit, and experience of a pro-fessional, savvy celebrant. If you are about to get married, this book delivers the all-important information you need with clarity, humor, and supreme coolness. His keen advice, direction, and examples are sure to make a wedding day the best it could ever be—for both the couple getting married and their tribe of family and friends. Shelley is one of the most skilled, talented, and debonair certified Life Cycle Celebrants®; he makes all his couples and their guests feel royal."

> —Charlotte Eulette, International Director of the Celebrant Foundation & Institute

"Shelley is the maestro of matrimony. He has been gifted with a divine power to imbue your wedding ceremony with off-the-chain joy. The kind of joy that starts your marriage off with a bang. Read this book. You'll learn at the feet of the master and have a ball doing it."

> —Jen Spyra, staff writer at *The Late Show with Stephen Colbert*

"I would love for Chris to be my celebrant. I say that despite the fact that I *know* it would probably just end up as more material for another hilarious book on weddings. After reading this book, if your questions still aren't answered about what goes down at a wedding, don't get married."

> —Jordan Carlos, comedian and writer

"A funny, practical, and romantic guide to why most weddings suck and why yours doesn't have to. My favorite work by a Shelley since *Frankenstein*—and ideally, when he married us, Chris would've sewn me and my wife into one person as well."

> —Daniel Kibblesmith, author of *Santa's Husband* (happily married to Jennifer Wright)

BEST.
CEREMONY.
EVER.

HOW TO MAKE THE SERIOUS WEDDING STUFF UNIQUE

Christopher Shelley

THE COUNTRYMAN PRESS
A division of W. W. Norton & Company
Independent Publishers Since 1923

Illustration credits, by first use:
Alyssa Roberts Comstock: horrified grandma, page 13; visionary director, page 14;
rings, page 16; chair, page 18; flower, page 18; bells, page 58; letter, page 66; fireworks,
page 66
© Joboy O G/iStockPhoto.com: double heart, page 18; dove, page 54; candle, page 96;
cake, page 111
© GreenTana/iStockPhoto.com: altar, page 25; mic, page 25; trumpet, page 31;
text bubble, page 54; champagne, page 58; balloons, page 111

For information about permission to reproduce selections from this book,
write to Permissions, The Countryman Press,
500 Fifth Avenue, New York, NY 10110

For information about special discounts for bulk purchases, please contact
W. W. Norton Special Sales at specialsales@wwnorton.com or 800-233-4830

Manufacturing by LSC Communications, Harrisonburg
Book design by Anna Reich
Production manager: Devon Zahn

The Countryman Press
www.countrymanpress.com

A division of W. W. Norton & Company, Inc.
500 Fifth Avenue, New York, NY 10110
www.wwnorton.com

978-1-68268-285-2 (pbk.)

10 9 8 7 6 5 4 3 2 1

To my wife, King . . . at last.

♥

CONTENTS

ACT V

♥

♥

◄ INTRODUCTION ►

Hello newly engaged person, someday-engaged person, smart wedding professional, parent of a bride or groom, friend of somebody getting married, relative of someone getting married, neighbor of somebody getting married, literate person who enjoys learning, romantic, entertainer, fan of wordplay, lover of love, realist, pragmatist, idea enthusiast, bookstore browser, or other. I'm so glad you picked up this book; it was written especially for you.

In the past several years, I've officiated hundreds of weddings. I keep getting hired because I keep making couples and wedding professionals happy. I make these people happy because of my unique approach to wedding ceremonies.

Here's a sampling of what people say to me at cocktail hours after they see me officiate a wedding:

"How are you friends with the couple?"

"Oh my God, that was totally the Best. Ceremony. EVER.'

"Would you like an organic tomato burger?"

Mothers hug me. Fathers grip my hand and slap my shoulder, relieved and delighted that I've set everyone into a buzzing-good mood. Brides and grooms express their thanks. Bridesmaids and groomsmen who ignored me before the ceremony slap me on the back. Other wedding vendors ask for my card. Guests ask if I'm free for their niece's wedding. All these people just saw me officiate a wedding ceremony in a way they'd never seen before, and they are so happy. This book is about how I make those people so happy, and how you can make them happy too. Well, not *those* people specifically; my point is that you too can make wedding guests happy.

Wedding ceremonies get a bad rap—for good reason. We've all attended dreadful ceremonies. We've all found ourselves sitting in a church, catering hall, or humid, sun-drenched field looking at our watch, longing for it to end. The stigma about wedding ceremonies is that they are the heavy things people must sit through to earn the cocktail hour. Somehow, something joyful has become penance. Wedding ceremonies are the vegetables before the cake. They are the work week before the weekend. They are whoever opens for U2.

Ceremonies have long borne the burden of being the final test for couples before they make their bond official, one last reminder of the seriousness of the undertaking, and an opportunity to strike fear into the couple's hearts. I understand why this is the case. To say that marriage is a big deal is an understatement; marriage asks couples to care for each other through good times and bad. Marriage asks them to make excruciating life and death decisions together. Engagement periods are romantic, optimistic, positive junctures for couples, when the road in front of them appears full of promise and sunshine. It may be easy during this time to forget how heavy life can be down the road. And yet I see no reason that families, friends, and counselors can't remind couples of all these things *before* the wedding day. In fact, I think it is downright irresponsible for people to wait until the wedding day to try to make couples think about what they're doing by getting married. If the couple makes it all the way to the wedding day without their convictions being changed, then that day should be a day of pure celebration.

I've always believed that ceremonies can be meaningful *and* entertaining. By "meaningful," I mean respectful of the seriousness of the undertaking and cognizant of the joy therein. I've been using years of theatrical training, extensive study and experimentation in creative writing, a DNA-transmitted wit, and a comedian's sense of timing to surprise hundreds of couples and thousands of wedding guests with entertaining yet meaningful ceremonies all over New York, New Jersey, Ohio, Kentucky, Arizona—really, anywhere people will pay me to go. I've been on *The Rachael Ray Show*. I've spoken at the UN. I've written and performed a memorial service for Joan Rivers' dog, on the late comedienne's show *Joan & Melissa: Joan Knows Best.*

I became a certified Life-Cycle Celebrant®, with a focus on weddings, through the Celebrant Foundation & Institute. This is a program that prepares people to create personal ceremonies for couples in a way that honors and celebrates all varieties of cultural beliefs, spiritual beliefs, and worldviews. I learned the art of storytelling, ritual, and cultural diplomacy. Celebrants are trained to bring people of the world together through marriage. The program takes seven months to complete and is one of the most rewarding things I've ever done.

Not every couple is lucky enough to have a trained celebrant officiate their wedding, so I encourage you to let this book get you thinking like a celebrant and working with the person performing your wedding ceremony with a celebrant's eye for opportunity. This book will help couples and wedding professionals identify the often-overlooked theatrical potential in every aspect of ceremonies. These pages also offer tips and advice for the person performing the ceremony—particularly in the aptly titled "Performing the Ceremony" chapter. Good ceremonies are always a result of a couple working closely with their officiant, so I will remind you of this often. Ceremonies are a team effort.

This book is a guide to all the usual wedding ceremony tropes and how to exploit the magical, unique opportunities they hold in order to create an unforgettable guest experience that still honors the couple and marriage in general, all while minimizing the use of snooty SAT words like "tropes."

Since I began doing this work, I've been finding inspired ways to utilize all available resources: the bridal party, the family, the scenery, the music, the staging, and, most of all, the love story itself. From processional choreography to Greek chorus bridal parties to harp solos to hidden choirs to "unity pretzels" from Fifth Avenue cart guys, I've made the most of every opportunity. I've married people on swank rooftops, in hipster back patios, grand ballrooms, catering halls, a baseball stadium, riverboats, gardens, hotel suites, parks, wineries, libraries, a library hotel, a train station, rustic warehouses, repurposed churches, barns, historical societies, one old retired cop's living room, and TV studios. All of these places contain opportunities to turn wedding ceremonies into unique laugh-and-cry fests of celebration.

One of the most frequent clichés included in clients' inquiries is "short and sweet." It is possible to have a unique wedding that is still short and sweet. A ceremony can be contained, spare, haiku-like in its simplicity, yet unique and inspiring. A Broadway singer with skill does not need a stage, a set, a dozen dancers, and fabulous lighting to knock your socks off with her singing. All she needs is a few minutes of your time, that special fire within her, and the bravery to let it burn your face off.

Best. Ceremony. Ever. details the inspiration found in every aspect of the wedding ceremony and shows how to incorporate loads of humor into it while still respecting the tux-and-gown gravity of this important transitional life event. The ideas in this book offer opportunities for a range of sensibilities and budgets. Not everyone can afford to have their wedding in a mansion, fill the space with couches, light it all with candelabras, and have the cast of *Stomp!* provide percussion music. To those people who can, I say: buy lots of copies of this book for friends who are like you. Not everyone wants their bridal party to enter while dancing and shaking maracas. But for those that do, I encourage you to buy enough maracas for all the guests, too. Not everyone wants to take the huge transitional step of marriage in front of all their guests in an interesting way. To those people, I say: buy lots of copies of this book for friends who are *not* like you.

This book is not intended to supplant any advice from the hundreds of wedding pros who distribute it; it is intended to add the ceremony to the conversation, to validate this part of the evening, and to show how a ceremony can be a springboard that makes guests appreciate the hard work of every other wedding vendor.

"Guest experience" is a phrase I will use frequently, and one you may have seen while browsing through the latest Twitter posts from wedding pros. Going to a wedding is a big commitment of money and time. If you've ever been a wedding guest, you know this, and you also know that it is totally worth it when a couple is right for each other. The event is an undeniable celebration of these two people you know so well, or whom you just met through your boyfriend. We've all been guests at bad, impersonal, haphazard, slap-dash weddings. The instinct to improve the guest experience is a good one. Ceremonies can set the tone for a positive guest experience for everything that follows.

I recognize that there is a generation of people out there with a passion for bespoke life-tailoring. Some would call this book a collection of life-hacks for their wedding. To those people, I would say: call it whatever you want—I'm just happy that you bought the book.

This is not about attaining the perfect wedding by providing exactly what is expected; this is about heightening the guest experience at your wedding by providing the unexpected.

Entertainment is predicated on the unexpected, and at this point I need to explain something very clearly: you don't need to make the entire ceremony some completely weird modern art meets vaudeville meets Cirque de Soleil meets stand-up comedy meets Broadway production for it to be unique (although that would be amazing. I would totally RSVP for that wedding right away). You can make a ceremony memorable by altering one or two small things here and there.

I use the example of a horrified grandma to show opportunities to be creative in a wedding ceremony. Grandma, in the context of this book, is a strict, humorless, by-the-books, imagination-free, know-it-all, terrified guest. I'm not sure what she's terrified of. Invisible social things are hard to explain. Maybe she's afraid of what people will say...maybe she's afraid of how your wedding choices will reflect on her or her family's good name. Believe what you will, most of these concerns are ridiculous. The only thing anyone should be concerned with is whether the two people getting married are right for each other. This is not Grandma's wedding. Grandma had her chance. So, in this book, you'll need to ask yourself about your own tolerance for horrifying Grandma. Grandma represents what everyone blindly expects of a wedding ceremony. Other people can be grandmas too: your parents; your godmother; your best friend Joan from accounting; Geoff, your least interesting frat brother; Phillip, the venue host. In fact, as you plan your wedding, you may be amazed at how many people want to offer you grandmotherly advice, telling you, "You have to do things this way!"

No, I say. *You don't.*

Examples of ideas that could horrify Grandma are noted with this icon: 😱

Now and then, a creative force within me surfaces, usually after too many espressos, and I generate madcap ideas that may seem further out there than the rest. These ideas are represented by this icon of a Visionary Director: 🏴‍☠️

This book is not meant to undermine the gravity of the huge life event that is a wedding, nor the importance of whoever represents a Grandma in your life; it's meant to prove that one can still evoke gravitas, while, to paraphrase the musical *Wicked*, defying gravitas.

I love weddings. I love them, and I feel like they love me. To me, they represent hope in the world. They are proof that love is powerful, that the joining of two people in marriage brings friends, family, countries, and cultures together in a profound way. Weddings affirm that life is worth living, that teamwork can create something greater than its parts, that détente is possible between people of all religions and political affiliations. Marriages could become the new peace treaties. (Worth a try.)

I love getting dressed up and being around people who are dressed up. I love to work surrounded by decorations. I love working with live musicians. I love being around people who are in the mood to celebrate. I love being the calm, kind connector between a nervous couple and the state of marriage. As a man who has been happily married for over fifteen years at the time of writing this, I can say with great conviction that the connection spouses have is worth celebrating. The friendship I have with my wife just gets better all the time. For couples who hire me to officiate their wedding, I feel like an emissary from their future. I cherish the responsibility to show them that marriage can be a rewarding undertaking.

So, while I may outline ways to have fun in a ceremony, remember that all this fun is only worth it if the couple is marrying each other for the right reasons. I may get snarky about some ceremony practices I find to be tired, illogical, risky, inconsiderate of guests, or in play for the wrong reasons, and I'm sure there will be wedding enthusiasts, traditionalists, and actual grandmas who will disagree with some of the opinions I put forth. That's fine; they can write their own books. As long as we all have our eyes open while we maintain and improve upon the traditions and rituals that surround wedding ceremonies, we're all going to be just fine. The wedding business is booming, and it will boom no matter what because love is bigger than all of us.

People who work in the wedding industry are among the happiest, cleverest, most motivated and friendly people with whom I've ever worked. I am proud to be among them. I have never before had a job where the processes of the work inevitably lead me to become a friend to the people who hire me. By the time I've written a ceremony, I know my couples as well as a friend would. By the time my ceremonies are over, the guests assume that I'm one of the couple's friends. How great is that? Why would I retire?

HEY OFFICIANTS!

Yeah, I'm talking to you. Most of this book is geared toward the couples getting married, but now and then I'll set aside some advice specifically for you, over here in this sidebar. It wouldn't hurt for you to read the entire book though, so you can anticipate your couples' questions—it's always good to know as much if not more than your clients.)

♥

I hope you find the ideas in this book useful and inspiring. If I could officiate every wedding in the United States, I would, but no matter how much I scrutinize my schedule, this appears to be impossible. So, instead, my goal is to at least assist and influence as many wedding ceremonies as I can.

Christopher Shelley
New York, 2018

ACT I

CHAPTER 1

. . .

Setting the Atmosphere

♡ ❦ 🪑 ❀

Let's begin by talking about things that are preliminary to the preliminary atmosphere. What atmosphere comes before the atmosphere?

You know how movies start entering our consciousness long before they are released? We see posters on subway walls with little explanation. Trailers start appearing in movie theaters, building up expectation; then full-blown previews appear during commercial breaks and actors start making the rounds of talk shows.

Now try to think like a movie studio bigshot. How are you going to introduce your wedding to your guests? Will you have a website? Will you send out invitations by mail? Will you send an evite? A Google Meeting request? A Paperless Post? A carrier pigeon? How will you tease out the info about your wedding day? These are all great things to think about and talk out as a couple. While you're doing this, why not build some excitement about the ceremony? Do you want guests dreading another cookie-cutter ceremony, or do you want to prep them for the idea that something special is in the works?

Lots of couples have websites these days. It's a fun way to gather information in one place so your guests can have it all right in front of them. Websites usually include an interactive guest comments section to encourage chatter. Couples post photos of their relationship, even videos. Some couples even write out their story for all to see.

I don't remember seeing a couple's wedding website that included anything about the ceremony other than the starting time. There's an assumption that everyone already knows what's going to happen at the ceremony. On the one hand, this is good because expectations will be low, so they will be easy to hurdle. On the other hand . . . where is the excitement? Where is the drama? Where is the intrigue? If I were a guest, and I saw a little teaser like, "If you thought you'd seen every kind of wedding ceremony there is—think again," I would be interested. I would make sure that I showed up on time.

Some guests actually show up late on purpose to avoid having to sit through the ceremony. I know because I have heard this from actual wedding guests, and boy-oh-boy were they bummed once they heard how great the ceremony was. Why risk having some of your guests lollygag in getting to the venue because they assume the ceremony will be dull? Pique their interest. Give them a reason to be early. In the end, this will help you, your family, and every vendor working that evening.

Don't miss our ceremony; we're taking guest experience to new extremes.

Okay, Here We Are at the Venue

As guests arrive, what do they see? This depends a lot on your choice of venue. Did you choose a catering hall out in Long Island? A rustic barn in the middle of apple-picking country? A vineyard lawn? A mansion's grand ballroom? An art gallery? A Best Western Hotel suite? A hip Brooklyn winery, like Brooklyn Winery? The venue will say a lot about the night you have in store for your guests. Every venue comes with a set of preconceived notions. Choose wisely. If you are craft beer enthusiasts and you have your wedding at a fun brewery like Rhinegeist in Cincinnati, Ohio, this sets the tone that guests are in store for an evening that fully reflects who you are as people, as a couple, and as fellow drinkers. If you are craft beer enthusiasts and you let your parents book a fancy country-club wedding, even though neither of you plays golf and in fact both of you think that all those golf courses should be repurposed into affordable housing, then the guests will suspect that the event is not genuine.

Find a place that speaks to you as a couple. Find a venue that accurately reflects what you reflect to the world. Your guests want to know that your love for each other is true. Your guests want to see truth in action. They want to see smiles and happy tears and pretty clothing, but they want to know that all of it is genuine.

As guests walk about before the ceremony, are they welcomed by informative and festive signs? Do staff members alertly answer every question? Do they even need to ask any questions? Do guests feel like they're in a weird, unwelcome space or in the right space?

So, by now, your guests are wandering around a beautiful garden, or chatting over signature drinks in a dark bar, or posing for photos with each other against the backdrop of an ocean. Your names are everywhere. There's a table with photo albums and a big sign-in book where all your guests can write loving messages for you. Great!

What do the guests hear? Music can accomplish miracles when it comes to atmosphere. Music cues up memories of happy days. A string trio playing '80s hits, a hip vintage band playing swing, or an accordionist playing anything at all, crafts a distinct atmosphere that allows your guests to let their imaginations roam. Music makes guests aware that something is going to happen.

If I could have a New York street drummer playing crazy beats as I entered, I'd be even more pumped for every wedding than I already am. I'd have them play low, understated beats as guests arrived and mingled, then I'd have them alter the tone and intensity as the guests are seated, then I'd have them crescendo into something fun and extraordinary as I entered and as the bridal party came in. I might even have a horn section chime in near the peak of this music. Imagine that Blue Man Group is the wedding band. Try to hear a wild drum solo in your head, one you can't help grooving to no matter who you are . . . you want to move, don't you? It's exciting. It's communal. It inspires heartbeat.

Okay, Here We Are in the Ceremonial Space

Chairs are a huge part of wedding ceremonies. Every single guest should be sitting in a chair during the ceremony. The theater of weddings, like any theater, has many chairs, one for each person, unless you choose to do some kind of casual thing with long benches, like in a barn or a high school gym.

First, let's look at how the chairs are arranged.

There is no law that says there have to be two rectangles or squares of chairs on either side of an aisle. This setup makes sense in a practical manner, as all the entrances are showcased by having the bridal party enter up the middle. Parents can easily be dropped off at their primo seats, and if you look at the whole thing from one of the ceiling rafters, the aisle and altar space end up looking kinda like a cross. (Which might not be everyone's cup of tea.)

However, unless you are a bat, nobody will see the space from the ceiling.

The chairs can be arranged any old way you want. There are no seating police. There is no chair Chairman. You can create two distinct curves of chairs, like a fan. You can have chairs facing each other on two opposite sides, with all the wedding action happening in the middle. In a super-casual setting, you can have people pull up and place their own lawn chairs in any old way they want, like at a fireworks show, or a concert featuring bands who don't book big gigs anymore but who still have payments to make on their ranches. The ceremonial area should be treated like a black-box theater: endlessly adjustable. You can have a few sets of chairs set apart from the others, so guests of honor can have their own special place. You can have all the chairs in a circle, with one or multiple aisles leading toward the center, the matrimonial sweet spot. Any celebrant worth their beans can play in the round.

 If the budget allows, get some divans or couches, rocking chairs, hammocks, or swings.

Some venues offer very unusual seating setups. For example, 632 on Hudson, in New York City, is the former residence of an art collector. It has a teeny, adorable ceremonial space in front of a fireplace. Above this space, one can look all the way, several floors up, to the sky-lit atrium rooftop. A staircase wraps upwards from the ceremony level, floor after floor, all the way to the roof, which has a garden, fountains, a Buddha statue seated in a meditation nook, rustic old benches, and views of West Village rooftops. During the ceremony, some guests sit on the same level as the bridal party, while other guests wrap up and around on staircases and lean on railings, looking down. When I officiated there, I wanted to lay on the floor, on my back, and speak straight up at everyone. Instead, I played both level and upwards, like an actor at Shakespeare's Globe Theater in England (or his Old Globe Theater in San Diego).

Couples who are extremely creative can create a labyrinth of chairs, and the bridal party enters in a meaningful meander. This kind of setup would be a better fit for a venue that is a repurposed anything—barn, warehouse, factory—as it takes artistry to reimagine a space, so staff working at one of these places would have to be up to the creative task of creating a labyrinth.

Does anything await the guests at their seats? Something to throw at the end, something to read, something to drink? Sometimes seats are reserved for honored guests in the front row; what about people in the back row? What about the middle row? What about every row? What if you could put something on every seat, perhaps a welcome message, so that every guest knows they are expected and honored? Nobody expects anything to be waiting for them at their seat; and if you are making the effort to surprise them when they reach their seat, what else might be in store?

No matter what your seating arrangement, the guests are going to wonder *where* they should sit. You may think that the answer to this question is: "in the chairs." You are correct, of course—but *which* chairs? I have seen many weddings start late because guests have no idea if they are expected to sit on one side or the other. I've seen guests nearly paralyzed with indecision halfway down aisles. Some traditions have the bride's and groom's guests segregated to opposite sides of the aisle, but even if this is the case, I guarantee you that several people will not be able to remember which is the groom's side and which is the bride's side. (And don't get me started on the detail that Jewish weddings and Christian/Catholic weddings are the exact opposite of each other when it comes to sides.) And even if they do remember, the couple getting married may not wish to make that distinction. No couple has an equal number of supporters on each side, and sometimes the disparity leads to embarrassing scenarios. The bride with ten brothers and sisters fills up her side quickly, while tumbleweeds roll through the only-child groom's side. How can you make it clear to guests where they should sit?

Signs can help here. Like exit signs on highways, a simple sign or two near the aisle can clear up any confusion, at least for people who notice them. Thirty seconds on Pinterest will give you plenty of examples of the overused "choose a seat, not a side" sign. (It's kind of the Pachelbel's "Canon" of wedding signs.)

Another great solution is to use ushers. Ushers are usually, though not always, male members of the couple's families. It's a great way to put groomsmen to work, and I'm in favor of any task that will cut down on the amount of domestic beer the groomsmen drink before the ceremony. More often, though, the job of usher is given to peripheral family members or friends who did not quite make it to the major-league level of the official wedding party. One day, they might be chosen to be members of a real wedding party, but today, they're going to get those guests to their seats! Ushers can clear up confusion, especially for older people who ignore signs or can no longer see them because of cataracts or an inability to accept that it is no longer 1950. Ushers can offer a strong arm for guests to lean on as they make their way down the uneven grassy lawn to the ceremony area. Ushers can wheel in folks in wheelchairs. Ushers can relay messages between the bridal party and guests as needed. (Why is Grandma sitting down? We need her for the processional!) Ushers can retrieve the purse that the mother of the bride will inevitably leave on her seat and then put it back there again for her five minutes later.

Whether you have the traditional and predictable setup of an aisle separating two sections of seats, or if you have concocted a labyrinthine Wooster-Group-at-the-Museum-of-Modern-Art seating setup, make ushers useful by shuttling guests to their seats so we can get the ceremony started!

CHAPTER 2

. . .

Introduction by Wedding Officiant

♡ ♡ ⌂ ♪

It's important to use this introductory segment to establish that this will be a ceremony unlike any other that the guests have attended. My brief intro is all I need to let guests know that this wedding will be different from any other wedding they've ever attended, that I'm a trustworthy host with a sense of humor, that I appreciate the weightiness of the event and am strong enough to hold it, and that I'm super-excited for what's about to happen. Have you ever seen a warm-up comedian before a TV show taping? It's like that, but there's no Q & A, and it's only about 45 seconds long—longer if I need to remind people not to take photos or engage in social media during the wedding. I'm my own warm-up act. It gets the guests in a good mood, builds an air of anticipation, gets the guests ready to focus on the couple, and, most pragmatically, makes the processional cueing idiot-proof.

It all begins with an entrance. Every ceremonial space is different, but usually, there is some kind of walk from wherever I have been out of sight to where the ceremony happens. I use this time as much as I can. From the moment I enter the space, from the absolute very moment that anyone can see me, I am ON. Sometimes this is as simple as coming out from behind a curtain, entering the center aisle, and stopping, just for a beat, to establish that I am not some venue person here to check on the runner or take a photo of the altar. I am here to get this ceremony going! (The book I'm holding gives it away for astute guests.) I enter, then stop. And I'm not talking about a dull pause—I'm talking about a stop loaded with bubbling energy, a stop that nobody thinks will last long.

Find the stops. This was drilled into me hundreds of times by my hard-core Suzuki Method theater instructors. The stop allows the guests to absorb the story which that particular stop is telling. Think of it this way: it is easier to focus on something still than something that is shaking all over the place. The paintings in the museum are not moving. I have to be still. I tell a story with my body. Stop. I make a statue that tells a story. Imbuing the stop with energy is also important: it is more interesting to look at a hungry tiger that is not moving than a block of wood that is not moving; that block of wood will probably not do anything, but that tiger sure might.

If anyone notices that I have entered—and someone will—I smile. Enter. Stop. Smile. I'm probably already smiling because I love my job and the waiting is over.

Then I go!

Then there is the walk up the aisle to the ceremonial space. For as long as I remember, I have spent this time saying "hello" over and over, greeting as many guests as I can with a simple hello. When I presided over the memorial service for Joan Rivers' dog on her show *Joan & Melissa: Joan Knows Best,* all the guests were in place for rehearsal, the cameras were ready, I was up at the lectern, I had just done my intro, and it was time for Joan to enter. This is what she did: she entered the room and stopped. Then she smiled at the sight of so many friends who had turned up. It was a full moment. Then she walked to her seat, saying "hello" to each and every person there, turning to each guest with each greeting. It was funny, it was polite, and it filled the time from her entrance to her taking her seat. I loved that routine, so I stole it.

I have not met many famous people in my life, so it was exciting to meet Joan Rivers, despite the sad circumstances. Like she did with everything, she made use of it for comedy, but deep down, as she told me later, she really was in shambles over Max, her favorite dog, one she'd rescued and given a home. She was polite to everyone before, during, and after filming, generous to everyone, thankful. I thought, *That's how I want to be with people if I ever get to be an old Jewish comedian.* (RIP Joan.)

I miss Joan too. Back to your introduction: what should be mentioned in this intro?

Great question! The goal of the intro is to focus your guests on the ceremony, to escort their minds from the million issues they may be thinking of to the important details at hand. The ceremony is the most important part of the wedding day, and this is the moment to align their thoughts with this fact.

How the heck do I do that?

Another great question! You're a natural question-asker!

How can you get someone to think about what you want them to think about? That could be a whole other book, and if anyone could figure out a foolproof way to answer that question, spouses around the world would rejoice. Here are some tips.

Make the guests feel good about everything. It has been well-documented in documents that people will remember only a small percentage of what you say, another small percentage of what you look like, and a huge percentage of how you made them feel. So, I try to make the guests feel good!

From the moment I hit the aisle, the demeanor I present as I walk up the aisle, the gusto with which I take the microphone (or just start speaking if I don't need a microphone), is brimming with excitement, happiness—in short, everything absent from a Radiohead song. I can't wait to get started, and the guests love that because, by that point, they probably can't wait for this thing to get started either! I smile like I could smile all day. I'm breathless with excitement. I try to give the idea that there is simply too much to talk about. I drive through the end of each sentence (more on this later). I do not belabor anything; I move from important thing to important thing, building the tenor of excitement until it is full to bursting!

I use psychological mentalist language tricks. I plant seeds of thought with suggestions. I prime the guests to experience what I want them to experience: love, excitement, beginnings, drama, tears, romance, laughter, food, dancing—using the words of the evening to focus the guests on the events in store for them, and off the fight they just had in the parking lot or the work they are putting off until Monday or their jealousy of the groom or indigestion from that gas station hot dog or the lyrics of that Taylor Swift song. I get them to shake all this off and arrive, with me, in a frenzy of anticipation for a wedding.

As with meeting anyone for the first time, letting people know my name is a good start. Giving a fun and brief description of my occupation is helpful too, because the guests may be wondering if I am a priest or a rabbi or a humanist or some friend who got ordained online in the parking lot just in time to officiate. I let them know that I am a trained celebrant and professional officiant, to let them know that this is my work, to assure them that I take this work seriously *and* that I'm the one who is going to make the marriage official.

As the evening's entire exercise is about love, I use the word love within seconds of speaking. It's also about celebration, so I use that word too. I tell them that I love my job, and sparingly describe what that job is: "My name is Christopher Shelley, and I love my job. I am a wedding officiant and celebrant, which means that my job is to marry this couple to each other and to celebrate WHY they are getting married..."

Then I outline something wonderful about what they have in store for the evening: the chance to reconnect with people they've not seen in a long time or to meet people for the very first time. Plus, I remind them that they will be fed and then they will dance! How wonderful does that sound? Pretty gosh-darned wonderful. And I try to sound super-excited about it, to make the guests believe that I myself am looking forward to the evening's events, even though technically I will be leaving after one or two beers at cocktail hour and I'll be home in shorts and a T-shirt drinking Carlsbergs and watching reruns of *Psych* or *The Mentalist* with my wife before the guests even hit the dance floor.

Then, by golly, I welcome them to where we are, zooming in like a Google Map—state, city, park, venue, and specifically the wedding of [couple's names]. Gosh, it's exciting! Guests love hearing names of people they know! And meanwhile, in some hallway, just out of sight, the couple hears the guests cheering for their names, and that makes *them* feel good!

Then I prep the guests for the very next thing in store for them: the dramatic entrances of the bridal party. It's so exciting. Everything is set. Sometimes I check off the giant wedding list items that have been dealt with over the past several months: the couple picked out a person to marry, they booked a venue, they found an officiant, they selected a photographer and a videographer, they enjoyed lots of free advice, they made Mom feel like she was involved, they selected a caterer and endured a rigorous tasting menu, they found the perfect florist, the perfect ceremony musicians, the perfect band for the reception; or they just picked the perfect wedding planner who did all of this for them while they binge-watched *The Marvelous Mrs. Maisel.*

Then I bring us right to the brink of the entrance itself: the musicians are ready to play more amazing music, the wedding party is ready to make their big entrance, and I've had lots and lots of caffeine. (I've been mentioning this caffeine thing for years—partly because it is usually true, and partly because I like to plant the idea of *caffeine* and therefore *being awake* into their brains in this subtle way.)

Then I declare the wedding planning to be officially over!!! Let the ceremony begin!!! (As obvious a processional music cue as ever there was.)

Wedding guests have this natural default status of silent reverence before a ceremony, which is really creepy if you've ever walked into it. This is probably because they are accustomed to the poker-faced buzzkill of religious ceremonies. My introductory section is also helpful for the couple and anyone else who is about to enter the space and who may be extra-stressed about the whole thing. Remember, the bridal party can hear the intro and the guests' reaction to the intro. If I can get the guests excited and laughing a little bit, if I can get them cheering and vocal about their excitement, the wedding party will hear that excitement and know that they are entering a warm, friendly love-space, instead of a dark, chilly tomb.

Then BAM! The musicians launch into the processional music, which leads us to . . .

CHAPTER 3

...

Designing an Unforgettable Processional

♡ ♡ 🎺 ✿

Most people see a processional as a solemn parade of dreadfully important family members and friends, underscored by Pachelbel's "Canon in D," or as wedding professionals call it, "Taco Bell's Canon."

I see it as an opportunity for a series of grand entrances by important players. Theatrical people like me love few things more than a grand entrance. (I'm looking at you, Bill Murray!) Everyone's dressed up, looking better than they've looked in their entire life. Processionals are star entrances at a Broadway show, the introduction of the lineups at an All-Star game, a parade of characters whom you actually know (or whom your date actually knows).

Processionals take one of two familiar forms, usually: a series of stiff, joyless entrances in which bridesmaids and groomsmen are paired up, or a series of stiff, joyless entrances in which bridesmaids and groomsmen enter one at a time.

But it doesn't have to be this way! A processional can be delightful. In fact, they can be so fun that if processionals got the reputation they deserve, more people would show up on time for weddings, and that would help every wedding professional involved in your big day.

First, let's return to our senses, specifically our hearing. What do guests hear before and during the processional?

Processional Music

I hope I didn't offend any of Pachelbel's fan club members (Pachelbellas) when I referred to his masterpiece as "Taco Bell's Canon." If I did, feel free to complain about me on your blog. I also apologize to the good people who created Taco Bell for associating them with such a non-taco-sounding piece of music.

Remember, there are no laws about processional music. "Canon" is one of the most exquisitely gorgeous pieces of music ever written. It never fails to evoke gravitas, and its reputation is useful, I feel, in grounding the guests' minds in the theater of a wedding. As every psychologist from Sigmund Freud to Lucy van Pelt knows, songs evoke memories of feelings. Everyone will remember how you made them feel, and if you play "Canon" for your processional, you will make them feel the way they felt at other weddings, which may have been equally wonderful. Or less so.

"Wild Thing" is not so popular for processionals. Neither are "Every Breath You Take," "Let's Spend the Night Together," or "It's the End of the World as We Know It (and I Feel Fine)." The Evil Empire theme from *Star Wars* is not popular. "Mambo No. 5" never caught on as a processional song. Neither did Paul Simon's "50 Ways to Leave Your Lover."

These days, "Canon" is being given a run for its money by Christina Perry's "A Thousand Years," another marvelous song for cello, violin, and piano. The Piano Guys' cover of this song is oft-played for processionals. Even if you are going for a unique wedding ceremony which, as I recall, is the whole point of this book, I maintain that a painfully gorgeous processional song like "A Thousand Years" is still a great choice, because whatever happens in the processional will be even more of a surprise and unexpected (that's what surprise means!) when played out against the audible backdrop of *expected* music.

It's important to remember that you should hear music at your wedding that you enjoy, even during the processional. You do not have to play "Canon" or "The Wedding March" or "Here Comes the Bride" or "Another One Bites the Dust" or any of the standards. There is nothing wrong with these songs; none of them will bother you in the slightest unless you are a wedding professional who has heard "Canon" too many times during one weekend. That is the wedding professional's problem—they knew what they were getting into when they chose to go into this profession. If they wanted to hear "Copacabana" every night, they could have signed up to maintain Barry Manilow's spray-tan.

Still, why not have your musicians play something else? Your string trio or quartet or duo or soloist is not going to sing any lyrics, so the song is just going to be evoked instrumentally. String groups these days boast repertoires that include classical standards, '80s hits, reimagined hip-hop, country, jazz, and juiced-up elevator music. When the energy and hope of U2's "Beautiful Day" leaps from those wooden instruments, the energy of the room perks up. "If the song is different from what I'd expected," guests may wonder, "What else will be different?"

Live Musicians vs. Canned Music

Live musicians, if one can afford them, are better than canned music. Live musicians make the moment yours. Canned music, music played exactly as we all know it and have always known it, is too easy, too evocative of whatever memories each of us personally have of that specific recording. Nobody has ever heard a song played exactly the way a live musician will play it in that moment—this is part of why going to concerts is so gratifying: you hear the song that you know so well played just a hair differently, or in fact very differently, than you've ever heard it played before, and you will never hear it played exactly that way again. The song as played that way, and only as played that way, will be connected to your wedding.

Plus, musicians can extend a song when entrances take longer than we thought they would, or if something unforeseen happens that delays one or more entrances. For example, a bridesmaid may trip, fall, and break her nose. A groomsman may slip off to the bathroom and get stuck in conversation quicksand about trains with Walter, the bathroom attendant. The maid of honor might do too many shots before the ceremony and lose control of her internal GPS. A flower girl may throw a fit. A ring bearer may choose that very night and that very moment to experiment with juggling flaming candles. You never know.

You can also use live musicians *during* a ceremony. Strategically placed riffs, chords, or embellishments can add to the surprise nature of the ceremony. Musicians love it when someone thinks of fun things for them to do during a ceremony, because most of the time it is the same old thing, over and over. If someone invites a cellist to riff out the opening chords of "Smooth Criminal" because it fits part of the storyline, that cellist will love his or her job even more. If you allow a harpist to play a flourish as prelude to a flashback, she will love you forever.

Even if you only add one unexpected musical detail to a ceremony—just one—the guests will wonder what might come next at every moment. *You can't do this with canned music.* It would be too tricky to splice a slice of the guitar solo from "Undercover of the Night" (best guitar solo ever) into the narrative of how the couple met at a Stones' concert. I just don't trust recordings.

The one exception I'll make to my staunch rule that live music is better than canned music at ceremonies is when the canned music is employed only at the very end of the ceremony and leads directly into a dance party, complete with hundreds of balloons dropping from the ceiling. I can say this with conviction because I have been in a wedding where this happened, and I felt it brought about delirious joy.

Entrances

How can we jazz up the processional entrances? Parents, best men, groomsmen, bridesmaids, maids of honor, ring bearers, flower girls, the bride—so many couples assign important wedding party roles to a dozen or more people, yet during the ceremony, they function as nothing more than window-dressing.

No, I say! Use these people!

The entrance order can serve a dramatic purpose, building up excitement person-by-person until the entrance of the bride, because her outfit traditionally is more impressive than anything any of the men or other women wear. The processional is an escalation of fashion, culminating in the bride's dress. In some guests' eyes, the bride is secondary to the fabric she's wearing.

Before I launch into a tidal wave of processional suggestions, I feel I must mention something happening backstage during this pre-processional time frame. Some couples do not want to see each other on their wedding day until the actual ceremony. If this is the case, at this very moment (really, all afternoon), staffers are doing their best to keep the bride hidden away from the groom, with sentries standing lookout at critical corners of the building, all the way from wherever the bride is hidden away to wherever the groom may be at any particular time. These staffers, either wired through walkie-talkies or using hand signals like troops invading a jungle compound, do their best to honor this request. (See also my Heisman-Trophy nominated section in the Wedopedia on the "First Look," which delves into the superstition of couples not seeing each other before the ceremony; page 158.) On a cultural note, most same-sex weddings I've been a part of do not pay any mind to this superstition, with the result being they spend a lot more time together on the happiest day of their lives. A lot of same-sex couples even enter the ceremony together, acknowledging in this action that they are together already, in the world. Me, I'm totally in favor of this. Wedding days are twenty-four hours long . . . couples who hide from each other before the ceremony spend only a fraction of that time together . . . couples who experience it together spend a lot more of that time together. My wife and I spent most of our wedding day together, and it was wonderful. Just saying.

Let's look at some options for creating unique entrances.

Grandparents

If the grandparents are ambulatory enough to be a part of the processional, I suggest they enter first, partly to show respect for their age and the lifetime of inspiration they've provided the family, but mostly because they need to sit down! While I am in favor of showing gratitude and respect to elders, I find it cruel how couples sometimes make their ninety-year-old grandparents stand for minutes on end waiting for the ceremony to begin, then make them walk down the aisle. If the grandparents are spry enough to walk unassisted, terrific! Let 'em do whatever they want as they enter; they've earned it. Grandparents of the bride come in first, then grandparents of the groom. I am trying hard not to encourage you to have them come in at the same time and race each other to their seats . . . although I will accept virtual high-fives from any of you who think that would be awesome.

Parents

Options here depend a lot on how the bride wants to enter, either with both parents, or only one, or none. (The only three options for entrances with biological parents.)

First, bring in the groom's parents. A few pages from now, I'll talk about the choice of having them enter with the groom. If they are not going to enter with the groom, they can enter together and then have a moment with the groom when they get to the top of the aisle. In this moment they share with their son, I think it's fantastic when they don't just embrace but do something really parent-like, like Mom wiping something invisible from his cheek or Dad handing him a flask, which he mock-discreetly tucks into his tuxedo pocket.

If the bride plans to only enter with her father, her mother will enter earlier. Since it's gentlemanly never to allow a woman to enter solo unless she is the maid or matron of honor, the trick here is to find a man from the bridal party or family to bring her in. Who could it be? It would be really fun to have a huge bodybuilder or Chippendale's model walk her in, making her feel extra special. If George Clooney is available, he'd also be an acceptable option. So would Channing Tatum. Moms love being involved with weddings long before a wedding is even a topic in the household; if she does not get to enter with the bride, give her a little revenge and make her entrance memorable. Any escort better looking than the father of the bride will do if a Chippendale's model is not available.

The Groom

The groom accounts for fifty percent of the wedding couple and typically five percent of the wedding decision-making process. While the groom may have an opinion on when and how he wants to enter his own wedding, many grooms don't even think about this. Some do; they are often involved in the arts.

Sometimes the groom enters solo, sometimes he enters with his best man lurking nearby like a bodyguard, sometimes he walks in with his best man and all his groomsmen at once, sometimes he enters with his parents. Each of these options has its merits.

Groom enters solo

This option gives the groom the most attention and the best shot at feeling like a rock star at his wedding. While the bride soaks up the most adulation and gasps upon her entrance, the groom's entrance is really his only shot at being noticed. Most grooms dress exactly the same as their groomsmen, so they are often indistinguishable. When a groom enters solo, he can hear the whoops and hollers of his friends and see their shining happy faces.

If the groom is a baseball fan, he's watched his heroes come to bat while a snippet of their signature song plays, a tune that represents their coolest self. If he wants, he too can have signature music play upon his entrance. As he walks toward the ceremonial area, he can do an extended routine of high-fiving with guests along the aisle's edges. He can be carried in by sunglasses-wearing henchmen. Depending on the extroversion level of the groom, and how much he wants to freak out his grandma, his people, and his family, the groom's entrance can be hard to top. I hope I live long enough to be a part of a wedding where the groom is lowered to the ceremonial area from the ceiling, or flies in while suspended from a really strong drone.

And any groom may secretly want to dance his way up the aisle, to let out his inner groove and pretend, for thirty seconds, that he is Ellen DeGeneres. (Another reason I love my job: I can do this in every wedding.)

Groom entering with his best man

Okay, we get it: the groom has at least one friend. That's cool. The best man's main role is to keep the groom sane, sober, and physically at the wedding, so it makes sense that he'd be at arm's length during the entrance. They can choose to walk in side-by-side or have the groom slightly in front, which I recommend because most of the time the groom and best man are dressed identically. Once at the top of the aisle, they can do a complicated handshake, a manly fist bump, or whatever expression of bro-ness they desire.

Groom entering with best man and all the groomsmen

Whoa, somebody sure is popular! Look at all those friends he's accumulated throughout his life! Wow. I'm sure not going to mug *him* during the ceremony! (I'll mug Grandma 'cuz she's so smug.) This option can prove that the groom offers the bride safety, because at any time, he'll have access to several tough, cool-looking guys.

An easy choice with the en-masse entrance is to don sunglasses and walk in slow-motion, *Reservoir Dogs*-style, which is good for a laugh anywhere you go, I don't care who you are. (You can even escalate this by having the bridesmaids walk in at normal-speed, passing the groomsmen, who are still stuck in slow-motion, and arriving to the ceremonial space first.)

Groom entering with his parents

"Aww, that is so sweet" . . . is what everybody will think when they see this kind of entrance. They will wish their own relationship with their parents was as good as the groom's was with his. They will rue the day they ran off with Alonzo to live in Peru selling tickets to his doomed Shark Tank Rodeo.

This kind of entrance shows that the groom is not an egomaniac attention-grabber who wants to enter solo, and it shows that his family is more important to him than his fraternity brothers. This might make his fraternity brothers upset, but they can exact their revenge during the reception speeches.

When the groom enters with his parents, it is a clear indication that he loves them, which shines a light on the parents in a way they will appreciate. It also suggests that they helped pay for the wedding, which is a super-duper important part of the whole thing. When else do parents get to be treated like royalty? Mother's Day is but once a year, and nobody pays attention to Father's Day, which happens in March or November or something.

This one is a great visual: the groom escorted in by beautiful, crying bridesmaids who can't bear to see him leave the world of singledom. They don't even have to be bridesmaids; they can be any collection of women. This one should be thoroughly vetted with the bride. If the relationship is as solid as it should be and the couple has a decent sense of humor, what a stunning and surprising entrance choice this is! And, fair is fair, when the bride enters, a gang of sniveling, depressed men can follow her, pleading with her not to do it. (I am imagining Madonna's "Material Girl" video here, only with straight men.)

Best Man

If the best man hasn't already entered with the groom, he can have his own solo entrance, during which he can simply walk in on his own, which is totally expected.

Or he can walk in on his own wearing a Miss Universe-style sash that reads, "Best Man," which would not be expected. He could dance in. He could walk in still focused on the wedding rings he will be responsible for presenting later in the ceremony, suddenly notice all the people looking at him, pretend to drop the ring, find it again, happy to avoid the heart attack, etc.

Some couples pair the best man with the maid of honor, robbing both of them of the solo entrance they deserve and sending the message that the maid of honor does not often walk in heels. The best man can also be put to use escorting the mother of the bride to her seat, if she is not entering with the bride, and if the mother has no sons or nephews to take her in. The mother of the bride can cap off the escorting by offering the best man her phone number or a cash tip.

For fun, grooms who have much younger brothers can switch the best man and ring bearer roles, having the little kid walk in all tough-like as the best man, and having the actual best man enter with the rings, dressed as a Secret Service guy. (Ultimately, the ring bearer can go sit down with his folks or legal guardians, and the real best man can stand next to the groom.)

Groomsmen

First, it should be a law that all groomsmen must wear outrageous, funny socks to weddings. At some point in the evening, the socks need to be revealed.

Second, if they enter solo, they should have free reign to spice up their entrances in any of the following ways:

- dancing to the music being played, no matter how light or heavy the music may be
- dancing in a way completely contrasting with the mood of the music being played—a salsa entrance to a slow traditional wedding song, for example
- entering as if they are boxers arriving for a boxing match
- entering as if they are runway models
- entering as if the entire day is for them, milking the moment
- doing a cartwheel part-way up the aisle
- skipping up the aisle
- jumping-rope up the aisle
- hopscotching up the aisle
- entering carrying a long rope (or miming one), pretending they are climbing a mountain (the celebrant can hold the other end of the rope). Then the bridesmaids can follow, with the groomsmen pulling them up the mountain
- skateboarding up the aisle
- roller skating/blading up the aisle

Third, when the groomsmen enter the ceremonial area, whether solo or paired up, they should all take a moment to have a moment with the groom, since he's just standing there. They could give him any of the following things:

- a real hug
- a bro-hug

- a much-too-long, don't-leave-me hug
- a high-five
- a high-five up-top and down-low
- a fist bump
- a leaping chest bump
- a punch to the gut
- a Namaste bow
- an overly formal Japanese-style bow where neither knows when to stop
- an aristocratic, Moliere-inspired farcical elaborate bow
- a good hair-mussing up
- a Godfather-style, palms-to-cheeks, double kiss of death
- a good tie-straightening with a solid cheek-slapping

Bridesmaids

Bridesmaids are hand-picked by the bride to stand up there on her wedding day, supporting her as she makes the huge transitional step of becoming married. They tend to be sisters, best friends, and under-cover therapists. One of the bridesmaids' biggest challenges is to look less beautiful than the bride. (Indeed, this is a challenge for the groomsmen, best man, maid of honor, and officiant as well.) Brides-maids' dresses are designed to enforce the notion that they are not the stars of this wedding. One can learn a lot about the bride's levels of self-confidence by observing the quality and style of the bridesmaids' dresses. These dresses range from not-the-bride-but-still-elegant to '80s junior-prom eyesore.

At most weddings, the bridesmaids all hold a bouquet of pretty flow-ers, which is, of course, a beautiful, classy thing unless they are allergic to flowers. Here are some other things they could hold:

- a box of tissues: people cry at weddings; wouldn't it stand to rea-son that somebody should supply tissues? They could offer the tissues to each other, to the couple, to guests.
- golf clubs, if the couple are golf enthusiasts and/or the wedding is at a golf club

- farm equipment, if the couple are farmers, or the venue is a barn; have one carry a hoe.
- champagne flutes full of bubbly; why assume everyone has to wait until cocktail hour for cocktail hour?
- smartphones: if you can't beat 'em, join 'em. Have the bridesmaids live-stream the ceremony.
- a pretend phone call with someone (*Oh my god, I'm totally walking up the aisle right now. Yeah, I can talk...*)

Beyond what the bridesmaids carry, they can have fun with their entrance too. Their entrance can play off the groomsmen's entrance, (see *Reservoir Dogs* example, above) or be unique to themselves. You may want to have their entrance completely contrast with the groomsmen's entrance:

- If the groomsmen enter with great decorum, the bridesmaids enter in party mode, dancing to totally different music (or the same music!). Once in place, either have the groomsmen get the bridesmaids to snap to attention, or have them loosen up and join in the grooving.
- If the groomsmen enter with wild abandon, the bridesmaids enter with elegant grace, to the same music (or different music!). Once in place, they get the groomsmen to snap to attention.
- If the groomsmen entered individually, the bridesmaids enter together and vice versa.
- Have the bridesmaids' entrance match the groomsmen's: see examples above.
- Have the groomsmen pull the bridesmaids behind them on a moving float (assembly required!).

Like the groomsmen, encourage the bridesmaids to acknowledge the groom in some way:

- a wink
- a finger-gun shot
- a fist bump
- blow him a kiss

- a wave
- any of the high-five variations
- hand him a tissue
- brush imaginary lint from his jacket
- straighten his tie
- straighten his hair
- undo the previous tie-straightening and hair-straightening

Bridesmaids and Groomsmen Paired Up

When the bridesmaids and groomsmen are paired up for their entrances, I always encourage them to take a moment before parting to do something to acknowledge that they've experienced a journey together up that long aisle. It's a real downer when a paired-up bridesmaid and groomsman just ditch each other's hands and sulk off in opposite directions as if they've just had an argument. This usually happens because nobody bothers to pay any attention to this detail.

Nobody would expect to see the bridesmaids and groomsmen do any of the following things as they part to their respective sides of the altar:

- a fist bump
- a high-five
- a high-five up-top and down-low
- a hip bump
- the groomsman planting a graceful, gentlemanly kiss on the bridesmaid's hand
- the groomsman, seemingly about to plant a graceful, gentlemanly kiss on the bridesmaid's hand, instead planting the kiss *on his own hand*
- a grand bow/curtsy
- a calm Namaste-bow
- the groomsman guiding the bridesmaid in a graceful twirl (or vice versa)
- the groomsman dipping the bridesmaid like Fred Astaire/Ginger Rogers

- a fist-clench/head snap like in Janet Jackson's "Rhythm Nation" video
- a brief dance move à la Travolta and Thurman in *Pulp Fiction*

Have them do something, *anything*, other than ditch each other as soon as they are supposed to part to their separate sides. When a motif is established, the anticipation is palpable, as everyone wants to know what the next couple will do when they enter. Ideally, the first couple does something small, the second something larger, the third something even larger, so the expectation escalates.

Maid of Honor

This is a rough day for the maid of honor: let her do as much or as little as she'd like to do for her entrance. She's been up since dawn keeping the bride from freaking out, and she's probably ready for this whole thing to be over. If she wants to enter with no fanfare, that's cool. If she wants "I Will Survive" pumping through the airwaves as she grooves down the aisle, that's cool too. If she wants to enter with a sign on her back that reads, "OMG guys, the bride looks good, don't get me wrong, but she has been a *total* pain in my ass today," that's her choice. Some clients insist on having the maid of honor paired up with the best man, and while this is an option, I always try to talk them into letting her have her own entrance. Maids of honor really do have a rough job playing second fiddle to the bride. I mean, the word "maid" is right there in her title. When clients insist on pairing up the maid of honor, they are robbing her of even that one twenty-second moment of recognition, so you can bet that something prickly exists in that relationship.

Ring Bearers

The broadest comedy possible is to get the kid to wear a giant bear head and call him the Ring Bear. I've seen it done, and I maintain that it should be done at every wedding around the English-speaking world. It's gold! Beyond that, who doesn't love seeing a little kid in a tuxedo?

I've seen them dressed up as G-Men, Secret Service guys with locked suitcases and signs like, "Ring Security," and such. All of these ideas are great. Truth is, you can just let the little tyke be himself, and the guests will probably find him adorable. Kids are our most reliable smile-creators. Just send them out there and whatever happens, happens. In fact, I love ring bearers so much, I'm in favor of having them enter first—get folks in a good mood right away! They are usually held off until late in the processional, but since there are no rules, they don't need to be. If they're difficult, maybe invite them to ride a scooter down the aisle, or a skateboard, or roller skates. Whatever you do, do not give them the real rings to bear. Give the real rings to the best man, unless he is also five years old.

 Couples with a dry sense of humor and guests who share their humor may also have their hairiest homosexual friend enter with the rings; he too would be a Ring Bear. It might be smart to have him wearing a sign that says as much if one suspects that some guests won't get the joke.

Flower Girls

These are the puppies-in-the-window of the wedding, the guaranteed smile-makers. Their one simple task is to decorate the aisle with pretty flower petals in advance of the bride's imminent arrival. The flower girl is usually the least-equipped person to take care of this simple task, and watching her try to do so is always hilarious. It's a little cruel, too, sending a kid out to do some menial Cinderella task in front of dozens of people. If the flower girl is old enough to handle it, great! If you enjoy traumatizing children, then use the most terrified little girl in your family as the flower girl. No matter what she does, we will watch with rapt attention.

My favorite flower girls ever were both grandmas. Totally unexpected, and they did a bang-up job decorating the aisle. That thing was immaculate.

A note here about selecting ring bearers and flower girls for couples who are becoming blended families—meaning, the couple already has a child or children from a previous marriage or relationship. I will write a lot more about this topic in Chapter **8,** but my advice here is to make sure you include these children in some way during the ceremony. Assigning them to be ring bearers or flower girls is an easy choice; and in those cases, I also suggest that, if these kids have the emotional fortitude for it, have them stand with the couple throughout the ceremony.

The Bride

Once everyone has entered, it's helpful for the officiant to invite everyone to stand to greet the bride. There's no real way to make this little part interesting other than to yell at them suddenly like Frau Farbissina in *Austin Powers* (*Everybody STAND UPPPPPPPPP!!!*), or to invite them to show you how tall they all are, or not to get too comfortable.

Then the bride gets to make her entrance, which is already super-hyped and anticipated on fashion, social, and familial levels. Brides don't need to do anything unusual if they don't want; they are already a curiosity.

> **Wait: can the bride's entrance be interesting too? Asking for a friend.**
> Of course it can!

Here are some options that will allow the Bride to contribute to the creativity:

Bride entering with her father (or both parents)

Often, the bride is already crying at this point. Sometimes, so is the father. To make this unique, flip the expectations:

- the bride acts totally calm, while the dad wails uncontrollably (fun likelihood: a bride and her father trying to pull this gag will literally forget all about being nervous)
- they both wail uncontrollably as they enter
- they enter laughing at something, then keep laughing

- the bride and father of the bride can keep it together emotionally all the way up the aisle, and then *at the very moment the groom steps forward*, that's when one or both of them loses it and cries. (And then stops, of course, to show that they are kidding.)

These same techniques can be used in any combination if the bride enters with both of her parents, which a lot of brides do these days. Just double the recipe.

Bride to groom handoff

A big moment in the wedding is the bride being handed off to the groom. Never mind how antiquated this is, or how much it makes the bride look like property. Somehow, the bride needs to leave the person or people who escorted her up the aisle and finish the journey with the groom—which is the symbolism of the whole thing: this is, literally, A HUGE LIFE TRANSITION. In this moment, traditionally, the father of the bride has a tender moment with the bride, then a poignant moment with the groom.

 Sometimes, couples request that the officiant ask who is giving the bride away, and then the father says, "I do, I'm her father," or something. We have some options for this moment. For one, the officiant can make him produce an ID to prove he's her dad. The father of the bride can have an overly tense standoff with the groom, maybe even ending up nose-to-nose with him, until one or both of them break with laughter. The music can come down in volume, or pause, while the father delivers a short monologue to the groom:

- a laundry list of serious and not-so-serious advice, like: *Don't go to bed angry; sleep on the couch.*
- a laundry list of faux-serious, specific threats: *If you hurt my daughter, I'll whack you with a six iron, unless it's windy, in which case I'll use a five iron.*
- an expression of gratitude for taking her off his hands: *I emailed you the instructions.*
- a back-handed compliment: *You're not as handsome or successful or*

as fun as the other guys my daughter dated, but on the other hand . . . hey, look at me taking up your time. Good luck to you.

- Or he can just whisper something in the groom's ear that nobody else can hear, but which makes the groom look terrified. Then the father takes his seat, leaving the groom shaking in his boots.

Another inclusive thing to do here is to invite the groom's parents to stand and greet the bride's parents too, then have them and the couple stand in a circle, all of them extend their hands to the center of the circle, all four parents' hands cover the couples' hands, then, pair by pair, they remove their hands to reveal that the only two people still holding hands are the couple getting married. This is a way of saying, without saying it, "Hey, we all brought them together!"

Bride enters solo

Some brides enter solo, and to those brides I say, go wild! Dance, strut, take your time, take photographs, live-stream, sing along to your entrance music, walk your dog, wear a parrot on your shoulder, casually carry a whip, enter wearing sunglasses then whip them off, enter on a chariot, enter on the shoulders of a dozen tuxedo-clad gentlemen, roller-skate in, skateboard in, do a snake dance like Salma Hayek in *From Dusk till Dawn*—whatever you do, make it yours!

The bride doesn't need to do anything unusual; brides are the brightest star of a wedding, as sure as night follows day. Brides should have total control over their entrance, and they should do whatever the heck they want to as long as they don't hurt anyone.

At this point, it's polite for the officiant to invite everyone to be seated.

More Fun with the Processional

Every single one of the bridesmaids and groomsmen can carry their smartphones, so if the officiant asks guests to put away their smartphones, guests have a visual representation of people doing that. It's sort of like when the flight attendants on airplanes demonstrate everything happening on the safety video.

On that note, the officiant can do a brief mock safety demonstration à la flight attendants, indicating the nearest exits in case a baby cries, the location of tissues in case a guest cries . . . the bridesmaids and groomsmen can contribute to this announcement with mime and object work. (I was a groomsman at a Disney World wedding once: the best man and all of us groomsmen wore those large white Mickey Mouse hands sold at the park. We did nothing undignified; we just stood there in our tuxedos with the ridiculous hands on. It made for amazing photos.)

Once in a long while, I'll meet a couple who is way ahead of me in wanting to make their ceremony as irreverent as they are. These are the times when I really feel as if the universe knows I'm here. These couples are a gift to me. In these weddings, everything is fair game for fun—and mind you, this is not to say these couples do not respect marriage or the sanctity of a wedding—on the contrary, these couples happen to be ten times as secure in their relationship as other couples, and they respect each other enough not to do a ceremony that is totally outside of their personalities. Couples like this are open to even the most random and bizarre ideas out there. For example, everyone expects to see best men, groomsmen, bridesmaids, maids of honor, ring bearers, and flower girls walking up the aisle. Nobody would expect to see any of the following walking up the aisle—be prepared to horrify Grandma (FYI, one of my favorite movies of all time is *Airplane*, which I saw when I was ten, and which shaped the way I think forever. Thanks Dad!):

- beer-hawker/peanut salesman from a baseball stadium.
- Santa Claus
- a paperboy delivering papers (*Read all about it! Couple gets married despite objections from every living person on earth!*). Provide actual newspaper with short articles about the couple.
- a cop
- a runway model
- a guy with a T-shirt cannon firing souvenir Bride & Groom T-shirts
- Spiderman

- Cupid
- a dog
- Cupid with a comfort dog
- a tourist with a selfie stick
- a tourist with a floppy fold-out map, obviously lost

One of my favorite weddings ever finished the processional with a gag, and the gag was entirely the bride and groom's idea. Here's what happened: I announced that now that the couple are getting married, out of respect for the groom, any men who still had a key to the bride's apartment should come forward and relinquish them since they would not be needing them anymore. One man came up, then another, then two more, then three more, then one of the bridesmaids, all relinquishing their keys to me. I put all the keys in a bag. Then I dug out my own key and put it in the bag. Then I asked, out of respect for the bride, that any women who had a key to the groom's apartment come forward and relinquish it since they would not be needing it anymore. Silence. Finally, the groom's mom came up and gave me her key.

One of the best couples ever!!!

Do we have to have an elaborate processional?
Nope! You don't have to have an elaborate processional. You don't have to have a processional at all.

The No-cessional

Some of the best ceremonies have no processional at all, especially if the guest list is very small (two to twenty guests) or if they take place in a space that is not conducive to entrances and exits, like a restaurant or a backyard. We gather, I get everyone's attention, we focus on the huge life transition/ceremony. No fourth wall, no dramatic entrance, no anticipation of a reveal. The fun begins much earlier for couples who choose this, in part because they don't have to stress over the theatrical artifice of a processional.

These small no-cessional ceremonies can still feature fun preliminary music, either recorded or live. The couple and the guests still dress up. The space is still decorated for celebration. The difference is that the couple is out there with the guests, enjoying the day and their company, maximizing their enjoyment instead of hiding away someplace. When I do these ceremonies, I let the couple tell me when they're ready, and then I take on the role of a street busker, arranging my audience in a little semi-circle, encouraging them to come closer so they can hear me. If we have fun preliminary music playing, thanks to a musician or somebody playing tunes on their iPhone, we have it fade out... and I proceed. (The most challenging place I've ever done this was Grand Central Terminal in Manhattan, one of the busiest places in New York City. We were lucky to have an NYPD officer help us with crowd control on the iconic steps. They had only a dozen actual guests, but by the time the ceremony was over, they had at least fifty supportive onlookers.)

For all the dramatic opportunities presented by the processional, it's all silly and unnecessary in the end. Once couples and families spend a certain amount of money on a wedding, they feel compelled to go through the motions of a processional, but with no thought to how it could add to the quality of the ceremony. And that's why you need to buy this book for those people.

ACT II

CHAPTER 4

· · ·

Words of Welcome

♡ 💕 🕊 💬

Weddings are joyous gatherings, no matter how many guests are present. The buzz of friends reconnecting, people meeting for the first time, laughter bursting forth, high-pitched reunion-hug greetings, the backdrop of music—it all sends goosebumps up the spine. For bridal parties, it's exciting to be hidden just around a corner, listening to all that happy noise right before they enter. It's especially gratifying for the couple to hear it because it reassures them that people are having a good time so far.

During the processional, the focus shifts to the bridal party and all those dramatic, fun entrances, but once everyone is in place, I love to turn the focus right back onto the guests, to thank them for being present. These opportunities to have loved ones gathered in one place are so rare in life; it is important to welcome everyone and acknowledge all the things that conspired to have them in that space to celebrate the couple. When the bridal party is up there with me, I feel as if my welcoming the guests has more weight—it is not an abstract welcome, it is me, as representative of the couple, welcoming everyone.

The notes to hit during the welcome are many, but the buttering up we do here is important in making the guests feel included, loved, and willing to witness something unique. Here are some of the notes that should be hit.

Thanks for Traveling

Have you ever flown across the country to attend a friend's wedding, then it seemed like nobody cared that you were there? Me too. Even the simple act of welcoming people will delight guests who are used to a dour atmosphere from the moment they figure out which is the groom's side or bride's side to the moment they head to cocktail hour. Make your guests feel welcome, no matter where they're from, what language they speak, or how many times they've been remarried.

So, take the initiative to find out where the guests are from. (Bermuda? Bahamas?) The couple may have given a list of locales from which they expected guests to arrive, but they may have for-

PSSST—HEY! OFFICIANT!

Yeah, I'm talking to you! Look, I want you to be great at this, okay? Do yourself a favor at the wedding: if you have some down-time, mingle with the arriving guests a little bit, say hi, ask where they're from, how they know the couple. Eavesdrop on what they're talking about. Was there traffic? Is there weather happening? Get the scoop on the mood, because it will help you connect throughout the ceremony. If even one astute anecdote suggests that you are closer to the couple than you really are, you will have scored a wedding touchdown.

♥

gotten late additions to this list. (Key Largo? Montego?) Welcome them state by state, country by country, saving the furthest for last. It's pretty amazing how far people will travel to celebrate love by drinking free booze and twerking to Beyoncé. (Down to Kokomo?)

If the range of guests' home locales is geographically varied enough to include other countries, welcoming them according to their home locale is even more crucial, especially these days when airport security is tight and some visitors wonder if they'll even be allowed to enter the United States. I never ever mention or allude to anything political in a wedding, but I do make a big deal out of the guests who have traveled any distance to be present.

Speak Their Language

If possible, I say a few words of welcome in multiple languages. Not randomly—that would be *latterlig*. Specifically, I welcome folks in their foreign language if there is a contingent of guests who do not speak English (or do not speak whatever the language is the language in whatever country in which you are reading this book).

It's helpful to write out a phrase in the appropriate language and say it. "Welcome to [Venue]! Please forgive my terrible [Chinese] accent. We are very happy to have all our guests from [Beijing] here today. I am going back to English now. Welcome!"

What Mode of Travel Did They Use?

Guests use many forms of transportation to get to weddings, so I make something of this, saving the guests who had the briefest journey for last. "Thank you so much for traveling here, whether you took an airplane, a freighter ship, a train, a car, an Uber, or a skateboard, whether you hitchhiked with a lonely trucker, or in a limousine with Pitbull, or in a vintage car with Jerry Seinfeld, we're just glad you made it here."

Thank Guests for Making the Brief Journey

If the guests are local, or if they're all from exactly one town, I thank them for traveling from all over southern Ohio or wherever they are from. "We have guests here from all over the world, including downtown Cincinnati and Mt. Adams . . ."

And whatever I do, the words "new" and "jersey" always seem to be funny together. Not that I always have to be funny. I'm just saying.

New Jersey. (Hee hee.)

CHAPTER 5

...

Special Thanks

Never delay thanks. I learned this from either the Dalai Lama or Pinterest. It's good advice. So, thank you for buying this book!

> **Is it important to thank our parents?**
> Hmm, let me think about that for a quarter of a second. Yes, of course!

Parents

This is a great spot to thank your parents. No matter how fraught the dynamics of your relationship with them may be in real life, if they show up for the wedding, then you must thank them for anything positive they've contributed to your lives. Also, often, your parents are the ones paying for most or all of the wedding, so thanks are very important here.

When thinking about what you would like to have your officiant say about your parents, ask yourself what they did for you during your life. Did they make it possible for you to live indoors? Did they keep you fed? Did they give you clothing to wear? These are things deserving of thanks.

Did your parents expose you to different activities? Did they drive you to soccer practice, or violin lessons, or camp? Thank them for assisting you with these first-world pastimes.

Did your parents send you to the very best private schools and bring you to exotic beach towns for vacations? Did you take sailing lessons with an Australian named Brian? Did they celebrate your sixteenth birthday with a grand party at a villa, complete with your favorite food, a waterslide, and a performance by your favorite band? Thank them for introducing you to Coldplay.

Conversely, did your parents force you to pickpocket audience members while they did their magic act at carnivals, driving you from town to town, so the only friends you could make were lion tamers, magicians, and acrobats? Thank them for teaching you that everyone is a mark.

Did your parents allow you to sleep indoors only on weekends? Thank them for prepping you for your career as a Park Ranger.

Did your parents push you onstage at an early age because your throat condition made you sound like Tony Bennett? Thank them for leading you to your career as the manager of a cabaret.

Were your parents absent during your childhood because they were Fortune 500 CEOs? Thank them for helping you see that being single-minded in pursuit of more money than one would ever need can make you a real a-hole. Then thank them for offering to pay for your honeymoon—don't worry, they'll forget that they hadn't.

Everyone's relationship with their parents is different, but regardless, if they had anything to do with raising you, you should thank them for it, even if you just thank them for trying.

Friends

Make sure you have your officiant thank your friends for being at your wedding. Chances are, your friends have seen sides of you that you would have preferred to have never been seen. Your friends probably guided you and helped you in ways you may not appreciate now, but you will one day, and you'll really wish you'd thanked them at your wedding.

We've already covered how important it is to thank people for traveling a long way for your wedding, but it is even more important to do so if the people traveling are not blood relatives. Friends had a choice. Friends could have turned down your invitation and made up any old excuse, but they didn't. They flew across the country, took time off from work, and dressed up in their best clothes for you and your fiancé(e) because they love you and want nothing but the best for both of you forever. Or they owe you money. Or you went to their wedding. Or all of the above. The point is, once you remove that familial link of obligation, it becomes even more impressive if friends show up at your wedding.

You don't need to thank them by name. You do need to make a fuss about them generally. Have your officiant give a shout-out to something local and unique to your friends. Is there a football team you all cheer for? Allude to some cheer for that team. "Go Huskies!" for example. Was there a brand of shot that you would do with them at a significant point in your life? Either allude to that brand or, heck, let's do a shot right now at the start of the ceremony in their honor!

Having a pre-ceremony shot with the couple can be a deeply bonding ritual.

Thanks for Missing an Important Sports Event

Sometimes a wedding can conflict with a major sporting event. You've probably joked about this with a significant other at some point if you have any interest in sports: "What if your team had the chance to win the World Series on the same night as your wedding?" It's an interesting question, almost as interesting as the question of whether Schrodinger's Cat is dead or alive. I'm going to call it Shelley's Sporting Conflict. Here you are, marrying someone who should know how important it is to you that your team win the World Series. I mean, that's one reason you're marrying her, right? Think of the comparative likelihood of the two situations: of course, she's going to marry you. She loves you, you're perfect together, you support each other, and you're best friends. Her wanting to marry you is very likely. Your team playing in a deciding game of the World Series is very unlikely. Let's go ahead and say that most weddings take place on Saturday night. Playoff games are often scheduled for Saturday nights. So, you've got the potential for a conflict. The game will probably start at 8 p.m., right around when you are sitting down to dinner, supposing a 6:30 p.m. ceremony start time. The issue may not even be with you, the couple; millions of Americans are baseball fans. Chances are, some of your guests would prefer to be watching the game, and if they have money, they may even have tickets to see the game or have bets placed on the game. (For my international audience: what if a wedding conflicted with the UEFA Championship? Fans of soccer/futbol are going to want to see this game no matter what. How dare you schedule a wedding during the UEFA final, or the Euro Final, or god help you, the World Cup?!) The only way to salvage any kind of face if you've made the cardinal sin of scheduling your wedding during a majorly important sporting event is to acknowledge it and cater to it any way you can. They can put TVs anywhere these days. People can watch games on their phones—and they will!

What can you do during the ceremony? I once officiated a wedding for a bunch of golf fans, early on a Saturday evening during the Master's Tournament. A handful of the most popular golfers in the world were all within a stroke of each other (I swear this is normal golf language) and many guests were wondering about it at ceremony time. I employed the help of the musicians, a brilliant and fast-learning duo called NY Ceremony Music. Anyone who has ever seen the Master's Tournament on CBS or encountered a commercial for it can recognize the music, a gentle plucking of acoustic guitar played over images of Augusta National Golf Club: greens, trees, sand traps, fairways, flowers, very Rich-People-Zen. The musicians learned the gentle riffs, and at a point early in the welcoming remarks I had them underscore me as I adopted the hushed voice of a golf commentator, thanked the guests for showing up for the wedding during such an important sports event, and updated everyone on the current leaderboard (which I'd checked on my smartphone moments before we began the ceremony).

(Most sports events last for hours and hours, while a ceremony is twenty to twenty-five minutes. The short answer to this section is, tell your guests to suck it up and get their priorities straight.)

Missing other important life events can go beyond big games or award shows. Grandma can miss her Pilates lesson. Aunt Paula can miss her book club. Your brother can miss sitting in the basement playing World of Warcraft with his online buddies in Sweden. Find out what people usually do during the wedding time and have your officiant make something of it if you want to. If anything, it's helpful for people to put things in perspective; it's hard to think of a life event more important than a wedding.

HONOR THE DEPARTED

In a book designed to make weddings more entertaining, you may think I'd just skip the part where we acknowledge the departed. The thing is, some of those dead people may have made the proceedings much more fun. If the person we're remembering would have been the life of the party, let's keep their tremendous spirit alive.

Maybe the late great Aunt Harriet had a way of bringing people together. Maybe she had a special expression she used when greeting people or thanking them for being present.

Maybe the late great Grandpa Charlie used to sing a song that would make everyone laugh, or cry, or both. If the song is the kind of thing he would have sung at your wedding were he alive, keep his spirit alive by singing it at the ceremony. As long as it's brief and relevant, everyone knows it, and it's guaranteed to bring a smile to people's faces, it'll be a great way to connect the generational dots.

When honoring the departed, it is best to do so briefly and then move right on to the love story. Still, if the couple have departed family members or friends who played a major role in their lives and they want to specifically communicate something about them, then do it! Let the couple lead you on this. Some couples only want to generally acknowledge the departed, without naming names. Some just don't want to bring up anything depressing and skip it altogether. Others may want a lengthy remembrance for their departed, especially if the death was recent and/or unexpected. Whatever they wish is best. It is their day. One of the trickiest parts of this business is figuring out how to communicate the fine line between appropriate remembrance and funereal preoccupation. Weddings are not funerals, but too much lingering on the departed can make them feel like they are. The only way to make this section celebratory is to highlight the most positive aspect of the departed person or persons, to remember quickly and fondly the kind of contribution they would have made to the evening, and then move on.

♥

ACT III

CHAPTER 6

...

The Love Story

♡ ♡ ✉ ☀

The Love Story is the part of the ceremony where, if you're at a wedding taking place in a religious setting, you'd hear the priest or rabbi or imam use his or her own words for the first time, telling anecdotes about the couple, maybe giving them advice, maybe thanking their parents for donating so much money to the church. This is the only part of such ceremonies that feels personal, and these moments are often too brief.

In the royal wedding between Meghan Markle and Prince Harry in May 2018, Bishop Michael Curry delivered a thirteen-minute sermon during which he never mentioned the bride or groom's names. His task was to deliver a bit of religious oratory, and he succeeded in doing just that. Mission accomplished. I am totally on board with him given that what he preached about was harnessing the power of love the way humanity once harnessed the power of fire. That was all great, but I wished he would have connected the whole thing specifically to Meghan and Harry. For me, it was a gigantic missed opportunity. He said more about the couple later that week on *Good Morning America* than he did in the sermon. That moment was the moment I am talking about in ceremonies where the person performing the ceremony can make the whole thing personal, to show us why *these two specific people* are getting married. It would have been great even just to hear why they'd asked Bishop Curry to preach on the subject he did. What saddens me more is that some people who heard that sermon expressed that it was the only part of the ceremony that moved them—I agree with them, but I can't help thinking that those observers had no idea what they were missing, how much *more* moving a moment like that could have been. I'd love to sit down with Bishop Curry someday. Man, what a great guy he seems to be. We'd probably talk all afternoon. I would have loved to have heard a speaker as passionate as he is make some of that sermon *about* Meghan and Harry, even for just one of those thirteen minutes.

When a couple takes the time to make a connection with the person officiating their ceremony, and when that person is a gifted, professional storyteller experienced with wedding nuances, the ceremony can swell with meaning and entertainment. A storyteller can propel the ceremony with a romantic narrative driven with enough humor to keep guests on the edge of their seats. What was only a brief anecdote in these religious ceremonies becomes the heart and soul of the personal ceremony. I'm not saying religious figures can't make ceremonies personal; I'm saying that they *often* don't, and that they should learn how.

> **Doesn't everyone there know the couple's love story already?**
> No, they don't. Even those who do know the story have never heard it told by a professional storyteller. Everyone loves a good love story, but when do they ever get to hear one about people they know? A professional can spin the story with a fresh perspective to produce surprising depth. Plus, are you going to tell me that you've never rewatched a movie or TV show because you already know the story? C'mon, son.
>
> **You're right. I've seen *The Notebook* twenty-five times!**
> Of course you have.

The whole strategy of incorporating unique theatrical touches and humor into a wedding ceremony is to hold onto the guests' attention in such a way that when the serious, important, heavy aspects of the relationship are detailed in the love story, the guests will be enthralled and not tune out because they feel they have once again been sucked into a cliché trap.

There are as many ways of telling a love story as there are branches of Starbucks, but a chronological progression makes the most sense and offers the best momentum. The story can begin with where you are now as a couple and then jump back in time to retrace your relationship's steps.

Fans of Harold Pinter's play *Betrayal* can try telling the whole story backward. That might be fun! It would end with you meeting for the first time. (And be a lot happier than that play was.)

This chapter is for all of you couples reading this *and* for whoever is writing and performing the ceremony because creating a ceremony is a team effort. The three of you need to be a writing team; Colbert is not hilarious every night without help. The celebrant is both the architect and builder of the wedding ceremony, but the two of you, the actual people getting married, need to supply the materials from the home improvement supply store of your lives.

I will go through the big topics involved in the love story in the order I find is most helpful to address them, but please understand that every officiant may have their own way of arranging elements of your story. All these things are important to talk about with the person performing your ceremony—you are asking someone to speak for a huge part of your life, and you may have only met them recently. For them to seem like an authority on you, they'll need to know a lot more than you would ever share with your caterer or florist. Later in this book, I've included a sample questionnaire which will help you generate material.

Question-asking is an art form; good conversationalists are always questioning themselves to see if they can find better questions to ask, aren't they? The truth is, the best questions let the people answering do all the important work. My questionnaire is designed to make it feel like I am just hanging out at a bar with my clients, asking them open questions to get them talking. (See also Questions for Couples on page 139, for the complete questionnaire.) People love to talk about themselves, but the more intimate feelings come out when people write out their answers. Each question is an invitation to tell me a story, in writing.

- How would you describe your partner to me, if we were at a party and you were not allowed to pull out your phone to show me pictures?
- Was there anything that made dating each other challenging? If so, how did you meet these challenges?

- What are your memories from the early days of your relationship?
- When did you know you were in love? Was it a slow build or a lightning strike?
- How are you different?
- How did the proposal happen?

How Did You Meet?

It only makes sense to lead with the details of the initial meetup. How did the wild, unpredictable trajectories of your two lives cross? One of my favorite things about weddings is learning this because I love chaos theory, randomness, and fate. I love this part because one small decision can alter the course of two people's lives.

These days, the broad view of couple meetups is broken into two camps: the people for whom the Venn diagrams of their lives overlapped in the real world, and those who met by using a dating site to do the initial vetting.

Couples Who Met in Real Life

Lots of couples meet through mutual friends. Lots of people get to talking at a party. One of my favorite couples met by chance in the vestibule of a building. Both were in the building trying to find the same party held by a mutual friend who had not given very clear instructions on how to find her apartment. They had never been there before and once inside the vestibule were faced with two staircases, the right one and the wrong one. They went up the wrong one and only realized it was the wrong one when they reached what should have been the mutual friend's apartment door, and instead of hearing party noises behind that door, they heard a violent domestic dispute in progress. The woman turned to the man and exclaimed, "Well, I guess we've been invited to one of those murder parties." The man wanted to marry her right then and there. He did marry her eventually, in a much nicer place than that hallway.

One interesting couple met at the man's rock concert; he is part of a

U2 tribute band called Unforgettable Fire, and he plays Bono. (Fun fact: their ceremony was held in front of a fireplace, which we referred to as the Unforgettable Fireplace.) She attended the man's concert, got to meet him afterward through a mutual friend, and they got married eventually. She has the best of both worlds: she is married to a man who looks like Bono but who does not spend as much time on the road as Bono.

A lot of couples meet at work because they are assigned to a project together. I married a young couple who met at a bakery shop where she had to train him to use the cash register. They got married—eventually. A graduate student at NYU met a woman who worked in the admissions department when she helped him figure out his paperwork. They got married—eventually. Later, he wrote a book about making wedding ceremonies unique. Some people meet in high school, never date until college or later, but get married—eventually. Some people meet in high school, date in high school, remain dating through college, and get married—eventually.

The whole point of detailing the way the couple met is to get the guests to understand that this whole thing almost didn't happen. The main plot point here is that *were it not for this critical moment in the couple's lives, the couple would never have found each other.* Often, the exact point in time when the couple met could have very easily passed them by—sometimes it even has an element of Hail-Mary suspense to it: a woman is out with her best friend, she really wants to go home but agrees to go out to *one last bar,* decides the bar is terrible, *is about to leave,* and just then a gorgeous man approaches her, devastates her with his smile, and they get married—eventually.

When telling your officiant how you met, be specific. "We met through my cousin" is not as interesting as "We met at my cousin's Bar Mitzvah at Studio 54 and got stuck there when the power went off during a blizzard."

Couples Who Met via the Internet

Did you meet via a computer dating site? Which one? Who approached whom?

Students around the world could do thesis papers on the merits and philosophies of meeting in real life versus online. Romantic engineering poses as many questions as genetic engineering. (Can stem cell research lead to better love lives? Can the "undateable" gene be spliced? Can we invent a robot Cupid?)

♥

People who meet in person in real life are often not even looking for love, whereas people who meet online are very much looking for love, for companionship, for a life partner; there is a premeditation to online daters.

Websites help couples weed out undesirables and find desirables by incorporating hundreds of algorithms and filters. The theory of this approach is pragmatic and economic. Many people claim they don't have time for the bar scene, or the library scene, or café scene, or dog park scene, or any scene where they are interacting with anyone. Yet everyone seems to have tons of time to sit around staring at their computers. That's where many of us spend time, so it only makes sense to find people where we already are; it's where lots of other folks are too, and it's something we already have in common.

When I first began officiating weddings in 2011, couples were reluctant to admit to meeting on dating websites, as if they were ashamed of their love-premeditation, as if meeting that way was somehow invalid. They preferred that I jump onboard their agreed-upon public story. Back then, tons of people "met at a bar," almost to the point where if a couple told me they actually did meet at a bar, I didn't believe them.

Nowadays, couples are very open about meeting online. They tell me if they met on OKCupid, Match, How 'Bout We, Plenty of Fish, Coffee Meets Bagel, Other Sad Sacks, Menopausal Mavens, Lazy Introverts, Might Be the One, Love Me Like My Cat, Digital Don Juans, Control Alt De-love, Get Mother Off My Back, Buzzfeed, McSweeney's, or dozens of other sites. (Not all of these are dating sites.)

What's fun to learn is what details of their profiles drew the other's attention. It is fun to learn about who reached out to whom—it's more equitable online, I've found. For whatever reason, the online environment encourages women to be pursuers as often as men.

SCANDAL

Scandal: the shocking things people love to hear about when they happen to other people, and that they secretly wish would happen to them. *OMG, she fell in love with her lawyer? Isn't that a conflict of love interest?* OR: *Wow, she fell in love with her ex-boyfriend's best friend? Awkward!*

As entertaining as a scandalous romance may be, the ol' tact-o-meter would probably explode if you brought up every single particular about your love lives at the time you found each other. A lot of people are reticent about how they met because they were dating other people at the time. *This happens a lot: love has terrible timing.* Sometimes it's necessary to gloss over these details, to be strategic about vagueness. I find it useful to acknowledge that love has its own schedule. I like to refer to this dilemma as couples "making changes to the personnel department of their lives." This is a graceful way to show the elephant in the room the way to the exit.

♥

Facebook is good for getting old flames together, but it's good for surprising get-togethers as well. I married two wedding photographers to each other. One had commented on the other's public Facebook post about heading to the top of the Empire State Building to catch some great shots. They met up for purely photographic purposes, yet ended up hitting it off.

I've married several couples who met on Tinder, the app based purely on looks and location. This app, to me, feels like the closest approximation to meeting in real life, when all people have to go on is looks and attraction. They still have to make the first move, they still have to meet and sniff each other, but the initial point of contact is the same as in real life—it just happens to occur on their smartphone.

Even after people connect online, they still have to wipe the low-sodium soy sauce off their chin, pop a breath mint, put their shoes on, and meet up out in public. First dates for Computer Casanovas are as unpredictable as first dates for people who meet in the real world.

Early Days

I assemble images of the early days of the relationship. I highlight the myriad adventures they've had together, especially if they've traveled to interesting places, or if their relationship developed and changed in multiple settings. The love story can become part-travelogue. The guests can take a huge journey in the course of one paragraph: "They skied in Aspen, hiked in Vermont, and learned how to play the didgeridoo in Australia . . ."

I assemble the verbs of their early dating life, the things they did: "They ice-skated! They built a house! They covered up a bank heist! They dyed each other's hair! They bought kale!" I cover a lot of ground in one or two paragraphs; this moves the story in a way that matches the dizzying whirl of new love.

Obstacles

Stories are always better when the happy resolution comes about after a prolonged challenge. It's always more fun to watch someone pole-vault unarmed over a barbed wire–covered wall guarded by snipers than walk around it.

What made it difficult for you to get together? Did you live in different countries, states, or parts of town? Did your parents not approve of the match? Was one of you in grad school and the other working an eighty-hour-a-week job that filled your bank account but left you morally empty? If so, who walked the dog?

Some obstacles arise from more sensitive issues than others. Illness is a tough one; while one or the other of you may have combated a serious illness, and only survived the ordeal because of the unwavering support of the other, the memory of that time is often too painful to bring up. This is another area where having your officiant generalize and focus more on the big picture is important.

Many couples were involved in other relationships when they met. This happens all the time because love is stupid. It's wise to have your officiant dodge this fact with the funky, smiling grace of Bruno Mars.

Many couples have a sticking point, like children (who, fun fact, often stick to things). One wants them, the other doesn't. Or one already has children from a prior relationship (see Chapter 8). For some couples, geography is a sticking point, in that some want to try new cities and others want to stick to where they are: if this happened to you, how did it work out? Did you stay? Did you move? How did the decision come about? It must have worked out somehow because here you are getting married.

Remember, all that matters is what got you to this point. This book is not called *Best. Marriage. Ever.* That might be my next book. (Sound of my wife laughing.) This is just about the ceremony.

Proposal

The proposal part of the love story is the most fun to deliver. Proposals are rich with the storytelling gold of over-wrought plans that fall apart. I always get couples to fill out their questionnaires separately, so I get their different takes on all aspects of their relationship, and the proposal is the part where the versions are always different since, at the time, only one of them knew what was supposed to happen. Or the proposer thought he or she was the only one who knew what was supposed to happen, when in fact he was the only one who didn't know that everyone else knew what was supposed to happen because his co-conspirators were bad at keeping secrets, except for the secret that they'd blown his secret, which they were very good at keeping to themselves and keeping from him.

I always need to decide whose perspective makes for better storytelling. Was the bride's angle on events a series of bizarre misunderstandings? Is it more interesting to detail the groom's elaborate proposal plan and then watch it fall apart? Can I jump back and forth between the two perspectives?

Grooms go nuts when planning their proposals. Grooms put more thought into proposals than any other plan in their entire marriage. (One reason for appalling divorce rates.) Grooms enlist professionals to produce videos. They hire skywriters to fly across a specific area at a specific time. They hire photographers in foreign countries to capture the proposal moment in front of the Trevi Fountain. They arrange for flash mobs to do choreographed dance numbers. The material is ripe for inclusion in a unique ceremony.

Proposals for same-sex couples are really fun because there is often a disagreement on who should propose to whom. Sometimes they do separate proposals, mutual proposals, non-proposals. In opposite-sex couples, the pressure is still on the man to do the proposing; in same-sex couples, both of them get a shot. Doesn't that sound like fun? I'd love it if women in opposite-sex couples started proposing to their men. They would have the element of surprise on their side! Put the man on the spot for a change. (Another opportunity for a thesis paper—gender issues and proposal traditions.)

Proposals are amazing experiences for both the person popping the question and the person being asked the question. The elation after a successful proposal is superhuman, equivalent to planning to leap over a skyscraper and then *actually* doing it. The guests will either have fond memories of their own proposal or still be dreaming of having one some-day. (Or realize that their own proposal was terrible.) Either way, sharing the joy the couple felt during that moment is a wonderful way to get everyone in the entire venue experiencing the exhilaration of love.

If the proposal was humdrum, dull, or pedestrian, sometimes I outline all the plans the proposer decided *not* to do. (He decided that a skywriter would be too expensive; he almost proposed to her in Tahiti, but remembered that Hoboken is closer; he almost proposed after a Broadway show, but he didn't want to steal Mandy Patinkin's thunder.)

LOVE

What do you love about each other? Get specific. (But keep it clean.) This may seem obvious, but it is a good way to ground the proceedings in the very heart of why all of this is happening in the first place. Love is the ultimate diplomat.

If the storytelling has enthralled the guests up to this point, and they are absorbing every word I say because they are primed to expect the unexpected, then this is the perfect time for me to evoke gravitas. This is the moment to be simple and true. This is when the guests need to hear the things that the couple love about each other and what they love about themselves as a unit.

This part is its most beautiful when revealed in contrast with the hurtling, breathless, creative humor of the couple's meeting, early days, obstacles, and proposal. By now, everyone has earned the right to bask in what is beautiful and meaningful about this entire enterprise.

A little of this sugar goes a long way, and a crowd of guests has the same insulin reactions to sugar as the human body, so I don't linger here too long . . .

Fun Facts

What quirks, fun facts, and anecdotes can I slip into this ceremony before I dive into the recognizable elements of a wedding? This is a nice time to bridge the well-earned seriousness with lighter truths about you. Do you have ambitious goals? Do you have a collection of stuffed animals? Are you members of a group of like-minded enthusiasts?

Readings

Many couples choose to include readings as part of their ceremony—for more information on why to add meaningful readings to your ceremony, as well as how to make sure they go as planned, see the Readings section in the next chapter. As far as the placement of readings within the ceremony, I tend to put readings just after the love story, before the vows and rings, so that the love story does not get interrupted. Just after the ring exchange is also a good spot.

CHAPTER 7

...

Performing the Ceremony

♡ ⟲ 🎤 🏛

A Kamikaze Voice and Speech Class for Officiants and Celebrants and Others Who Don't Have Time to Get a BFA in Acting

Up to this point, I've addressed writing the ceremony, but what about performing it?

Without turning this into a performance conservatory experience, here are a few tips for whoever may be officiating the ceremony. If you are a couple at the stage of deciding who should officiate your ceremony, here are some things to consider about your candidates. Can whomever you're considering do all the following things?

Speak up. Even if you have a microphone. Volume implies confidence. (Screaming implies that your girlfriend just told you that her mother is coming to visit.) Warm up your voice. Use whatever vocal training you've ever had.

Lay the images out on a silver platter for all to see. No need to rush or bleed lines into each other. You took the time to write these images, thoughts, and anecdotes for people—make sure they do not have to work to keep up with you. Which words are the MOST IMPORTANT in a sentence? Are the images CLEAR or are they justajumbleofreallyhastilyspokenwordsnobodycanunderstand?

Writing for public speaking is different than writing for reading; short sentences help clarify images for the listeners and ensure that pauses are well placed for you, the speaker. It may be helpful to print out the text of a great speech, then watch a video or at least listen to a recording of the person delivering the actual speech, if one is available. (I am a big fan of the

> **OFFICIANT, TAKE NOTICE!**
> ....
> This section can help you perform the ceremony. I spent years of my life training to be a professional performer so that you won't have to. You're welcome.
>
> ♥

late monologist Spalding Gray; some of his works are available both on video and in print. *Swimming to Cambodia, Gray's Anatomy, Monsters in a Box*, and *Terrors of Pleasure* all demonstrate his mastery of storytelling—and he did it all just sitting at his desk.)

Write to your voice. Meaning, write the way you speak. The only way to find this out is to write something, say it out loud, and determine if your mouth feels comfortable saying the words as written. If not, change a word or two. It may be easier to say, "They got engaged in France a month ago" than to say, "Our frightfully delightful couple became affianced in France in February."

Enunciate. When you rehearse, saying the words out loud, can you hear each word, each vowel, and each consonant? (Because if you can't hear the words, and you are right next to your mouth, how will the guests hear the words?) How do the words feel as your mouth forms them? How does each letter feel? Do the words feel or sound like their meaning? Do any of the consonants or vowel sounds repeat word after word? Do they repeat randomly or for a reason?

Rehearse. Get your eyes used to seeing the words, get your mouth used to saying the words, get your brain used to the overall story so even if you waver for a moment, you will still always be at the right wedding talking about the right people. Rehearse with the knowledge that the words may come out differently in the actual wedding and that's okay. Rehearse with flexibility and openness. Rehearse in a way that familiarizes you with the text but does not make you beholden to a certain line delivery. (One must rehearse in order not to sound rehearsed.) Sometimes I rehearse in different accents, which forces me to really pay attention to the words, to consciously feel every vowel and every consonant. (I also work alone most of the time, so I need to entertain myself.) This also ensures that the actual wedding will sound different than the rehearsal.

Rehearsing is also useful to find the treasure of moments, pacing, and imagery in your text. Speaking of pacing . . .

Vary the pacing. Some parts of the story need to be told slowly to set the scene; others can be told in a rush of excitement. Never sacrifice clarity or enunciation, but if you can learn to vary the delivery of the dramatic and comedic elements of the story, your listeners will not fall into a hypnotic lull. Telling a story in which every sentence sounds like every other sentence is a storytelling no-no. Vary the pace and the tone. Clearly separate one part of the story from another by shifting gears, shifting position, shifting attitude, shifting narrative voice, or shifting focus. Stop completely sometimes. Imply the end of a section with sudden silence. Remember: stops are powerful tools in storytelling. While the words can stop for a moment, the energy must continue: just because there is a period at the end of a sentence, that is no excuse for the energy to drop out of the sentence; if the writing is good enough, the last word in a sentence is the most important word in the sentence and must be presented in the most accessible and energized way possible. Deflating a line's energy at the end of each sentence derails all momentum. (This makes the story feel as if it is hiding behind a couch when instead it should be bursting out of a cake.) Professional speakers drive their points through their audience's brains (like a Miley Cyrus wrecking ball).

Now I'm imagining Miley Cyrus officiating a wedding from her wrecking ball. You're welcome.

And this is *not* to suggest bringing the inflection up the way one would when asking a question. (Unless you are asking a question?) Vocally adding question marks at the end of a sentence or even *within* a sentence implies that the speaker is not sure that the listener understands what has been said—which implies that the speaker may not have said it very well, which implies lack of conviction, which undermines everything the speaker says and makes the speaker sound like a nervous fourteen-year-old: "Then Jimmy? Who thought she was a vegetarian? Took her to an Indian place? But then the food they ate? Was too spicy? So, he sweat like a sumo wrestler in a Bikram Yoga class? So, it was amazing that he got a second date with her?"

Give voice to the voices within the quotation marks. Do you quote people in the love story? Let's hear their actual voices. If you are a voice mimic, and you know what the speakers sound like, go for it! If you don't know, at least make it clear that they are two different people talking. Use your body; be one person speaking to the other, then turn to embody the other speaking back. These two people may be on the same level, like two people on barstools at a bar or standing next to each other; they may be on two different levels, one on a balcony, one in the front yard below. One may be tall, the other short; make this clear, and the guests' brains will fill in the rest.

Accents. Yes, accents! If you can do accents, you are in an elite corps of linguistic specialists. Use accents to catch people off guard, to portray speakers who themselves have accents, to expose regionalisms, and make the most of their contrasts. As I mentioned, I rehearse in different accents, partly to notice every sound the script demands that I make, partly to keep up with accents in case the opportunity arises to impress a hundred Australians.

Use every sense. Sight, sound, smell, touch, taste. Everything the celebrant does, indeed everything a storyteller does when telling a story is to make the invisible visible, the intangible tangible, the unclear clear. And all of this goes a long way toward evoking emotions (or as the kids call them, "the feels").

All of it goes toward making the ceremony personal, meaningful, and complete.

Readings

Many couples feel compelled to incorporate readings into their ceremonies—I have a lot to say about this. The smartest, most popular, and most logical way to involve a friend in the ceremony, other than to have that friend become a part of the wedding party, is to have them do a reading (see also Wedopedia: Readings and Wedopedia: Friends). Readings in religious ceremonies are often the only part of the ceremony with any personal connection to the couple, and to have a friend do the reading makes it even more personal. Readings in any kind of ceremony offer a solution to one of the stickiest wedding quandaries: what to do with that friend who means a lot to you, but not enough to make part of the wedding party? Have them do a reading. The guests' familiarity with the friend will be comforting, and this choice does not burden the friend with taking on the entire ceremony.

Readings in and of themselves can add a philosophical and/or spiritual color to the ceremony; they can be an extension of the couple's personality and shared beliefs. Readings can come from many different sources: novels, poems, song lyrics, movie dialogue, great orators, or landmark Supreme Court rulings (same-sex marriage ceremonies often include portions of Justice Anthony Kennedy's words regarding the legalizing of same-sex marriage throughout the United States).

Religious readings can solve two problems in one go: couples can have a friend or member of their family (or multiple friends and family members) do a religious reading to acknowledge, in an otherwise nonreligious ceremony, a religion or religions that have played a role in their lives, whatever those religions may be. Religious readings satisfy the dual quandaries of involving a person or persons who would otherwise not be involved in the wedding, and it fulfills the "my family really wants us to acknowledge their/our religion" expectation.

However, readings can pose aesthetic and theatrical risks. The effect of a reader's reading can be antithetical to the couple's intended effect—the reality is that not everyone is suited to public speaking; not everyone is comfortable in front of a crowd; not everyone is good at reading prepared text, no matter how outgoing they may be in real life or how extroverted they may be in casual public situations. Reading out loud is a skill taught to very few people these days. The likeliest to handle the task well are trained actors, teachers, CEOs accustomed to giving presentations to shareholders, and politicians (well ... *some* politicians). If the couple has nobody among their guests, friends, or family who are trained in public speaking, they run the risk of a really bad reading that can be a blot on an otherwise great ceremony, like a splotch of spilled mustard on the Mona Lisa.

Good readers make sure we hear every word and maintain the energy that the celebrant has created. Good readings are brief, perhaps a minute, maybe a minute and a half. One reading is optimal, two readings, especially if they contrast in tone, are okay. My favorite couple ever used three readings—a poetic reading, a Biblical reading that had been read at every family event going back generations, and one highly comedic reading, read by a highly comedic person. All three added to the ceremony, maintained the mood, and were in keeping with the larger reality of a couple with a wide spectrum of family, friends, and spiritual beliefs.

Readings can be great, but beware of having a reading just for the sake of having a reading; they are completely optional. When a trained, experienced celebrant performs a ceremony, it is already intensely personal, which makes readings extraneous. The usual thinking in more impersonal ceremonies is: "This person does not know us at all, so here is some source material that we feel relates to us as humans," whereas with celebrant-led ceremonies, the thinking becomes: "Here is a beautiful and personal ceremony told by someone who has really taken the time to get to know us, reading the words that we worked on with him—we find no reason to slow down the proceedings with outside source material written by someone like Shakespeare who obviously never knew us."

To sum up, choose the reader wisely. It's also a good idea to introduce the reader to your celebrant beforehand so the celebrant can provide some speaking tips, even if only in the particulars of using the microphone. It is best to print the reading in a large font and on actual paper, so it can be read without corrective eyewear, if possible. It's also helpful to have multiple copies of the reading available, in case the reader leaves his or her copy someplace else.

ACT IV

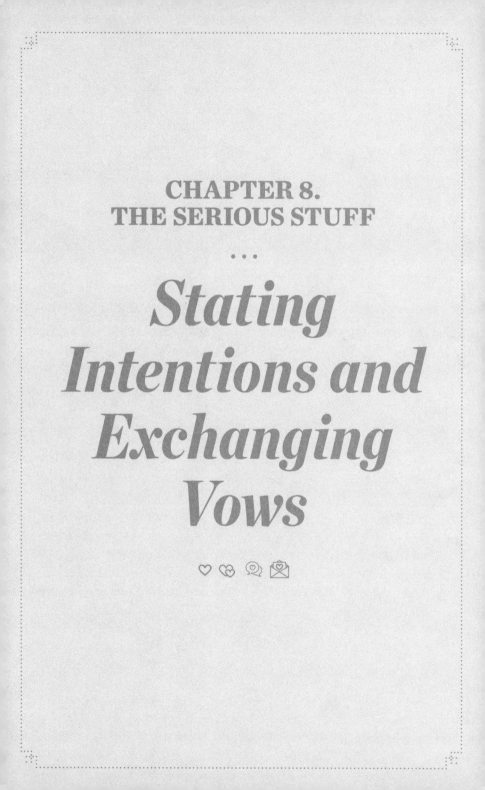

CHAPTER 8.
THE SERIOUS STUFF

. . .

Stating Intentions and Exchanging Vows

Whenever anyone sits in an exit row on an airplane, the flight attendants need to get a verbal "yes" confirmation that they are willing to help in an emergency. Even though they know everyone is just in that row for the extra legroom, they still need those passengers to *state their intentions* to be a good person, to help rip out the emergency door and direct people onto the raft that will glide them smoothly off the plane and into the ocean, hopefully not straight into the mouth of a shark.

In this metaphorical flight, the couple are the passengers, and the officiant is the flight attendant. And, in a way, a marriage *is* a wonderful journey from point A to points, B, C, and beyond, complete with dramatic scenery and the occasional emergency. The flight attendant and officiant are in charge of making sure the passengers and the couple are aware of the potentially serious consequences of joining together in air travel and in life. If the couple is getting married on the airplane during a flight, in an exit row, getting the couple to state their intentions is extra important. And, as always, if the seatbelt sign is lit, please do not get married.

Intentions

Within every wedding ceremony, at some point, you're required to reassure everyone present that you are serious about being married; you need to state your intentions. Not all your intentions—nobody cares if you *intend* to fund an organic fair-trade coffee plantation in Venezuela (except the Venezuelans)—all we care about that day are your intentions to love each other, to be faithful and honest with each other until death do you part. We want to know that you are entering into this never-ending live-action documentary of your love life of your own free will and that you are not doing this because you lost a bet to a guy at an all-night laundromat during a drunken night on the town, and now you have to get married to this drifter whom nobody seems to know just because a bet's a bet. Facts like that really put a damper on celebrations. The guests want to hear that you genuinely want to get married.

Sometimes this is accomplished using something called a "charge to the couple." (Also, how I refer to my fee.) The officiant lays out for the couple what being married means. By extension, all the guests get to learn what being married means too. Couple-charging can be a separate, brief moment in the ceremony or it can be elicited during the exchange of vows. Here is one way a "charge to the couple" can sound:

[Spouse A] and [Spouse B], until now, you have followed the unique paths of your lives, and those two paths have led you towards each other. Today, you will officially begin following a new path together. Many adventures await you. Years of happiness await you. Both of you are strong individuals, but together you will be unstoppable. Marriage gives you an advantage because a spouse is many things: a spouse is a guide, a teacher, a sounding wall, a consigliere, a court jester, a financial analyst, a personal trainer, a nutritionist, a travel planner, a dreamer, and a friend. According to several trusted medical journals, marriage is good for your heart, your cholesterol, your mood levels, your sleep patterns, and your skin. Marriage is a good choice. It is a deeply personal choice. It is a life-changing choice. It is a choice you make together, with a steady mind and a true heart. By marrying each other, you are committing your lives to each other today, tomorrow, right through the weekend, all next week, and forever. This is a choice to be made with all the seriousness in the world until there is no seriousness left.

You may have heard a rumor that there is something specific that must be said during a wedding to make it legal. This is a myth. As much as I would love to spread the rumor that the specific sentence "I promise from the bottom of my heart that I will buy *Best. Ceremony. Ever.* for at least five people in my social circle" must be uttered at every wedding to make the marriage legal, it's just not true. I hate to disappoint purists, but the only thing that makes the wedding legal is the signatures on the marriage license. The rest is for show. The thing is, your officiant should not sign your marriage license if they don't believe you should be married; the wedding ceremony, therefore, is a great way to convince the person who needs to sign your license that they should actually sign it.

Exchange of Vows

Most of the vows should be expressions of serious intentions, but there are ways to make this section surprising while keeping it truthful. The truth is that humor comes from truth, and truth can come from specificity. (And specificity comes from one exact place.) Vows that are broad, cliché-driven, and non-specific to the couple may sound serious, but without making a specific connection to the two actual human beings getting married, they can ring hollow. I push my couples to personalize their vows, thus creating gravitas from truthful specificity. The contrast of gravity and humor is where entertainment lives.

Some couples write their own vows that they read to each other. Other couples like to repeat often-heard vows to each other, whether they are the same ones their parents said to each other when they got married, or their favorite movie stars said to each other when their characters got married in a movie. Others prefer to do something called The Asking so that all they have to do is say "I do" in response to their officiant's questions. Others choose to do a combination of these choices. No matter what couples choose to do, this is a good time for the bride to hand her bouquet of flowers over to her maid of honor if she has not already. If the bride is going to be holding on to anything at this point, it ought to be the groom's hands. (Some brides hand their bouquet off as soon as they arrive in the ceremonial space. Other brides don't know what to do with their hands during the ceremony, so they choose to hold onto the bouquet a while longer—and why not? The florist put a lot of work into that bouquet.)

Personal Vows

I am one-hundred percent in favor of couples writing and saying their own personal, unique vows to each other. To me, it is in keeping with the entire ceremony to hear the specific things you have decided to promise your life- and afterlife-long partner. If you've made the effort to tend to every other detail of your wedding to ensure that it is unique to you, why stop at the vows?

My couples and I always end up talking about vows because part of my service is helping couples write their own. (See also Wedding Vow Workshop on page 147.) I explain the importance of this exercise even if they never intend to say them at the wedding. Some people are not public speakers by any stretch of the imagination and are afraid that the emotions of the day will overwhelm them. For these people, I explain that the very act of writing their vows is an important one for them in their relationship. It's difficult to think of what you would promise another human being. (I promise to think about what I would think about promising you.) It's really difficult to state these things efficiently. I maintain that it *should* be difficult, and it should be tried.

Even if couples are adamant about not saying personal vows in the ceremony, I encourage them to write them anyway, then to share them with each other privately, maybe after the ceremony or on the honeymoon. This is as close as I come to engaging in premarital counseling, something I am so totally not at all qualified legally to do. I mean, I can offer advice all day long (and I would love to charge money for doing so), but I wouldn't call it premarital counseling because I don't want to go to jail. (Wedding jail: endless "Canon in D.")

Many couples share my belief that personal vows are the way to go. I help these couples write them separately, so they don't hear each other's before the big day. As the only person who knows what each set of promises is, I am the arbiter of tone and length. I help smooth out the writing, brainstorm, rearrange, and balance humorous parts and serious parts. It's a pleasure to work with couples this way, an honor to assist them with the most personal moment of the entire enterprise. (Unless they wait until the night before to ask me to help.)

Some couples don't want to say personal vows because they are afraid that they will cry in front of all their people. I get this—vulnerability requires bravery, and a lot of people don't have the emotional armor to pull this off. I choked up while saying my own vows, but I persevered. It was worth it. My wife and I personalized our ceremony down to the last inch, and both of us are writers, so there was no way we were going to generalize our vows. It's true that couples may cry when they read their vows, but I maintain that crying is good. Real emotions are powerful things to share because they are genuine, and it is rare in life to witness anything genuine.

Still, this is too scary a prospect for many couples. There is probably a psychological term for the fear of speaking in public (menotalkaphobia?). If it is something so horrifying that it is going to ruin your wedding experience, then skip it.

Repeating Standard Vows That Somebody Else Wrote a Long Time Ago for a Wedding Far, Far Away

There are many options for this, easily found on the internet. Phrases like "till death do us part," "to have and to hold," "for richer, for poorer," "lawfully wedded wife," etc. are forever embedded in the wedding lexicon, and that's fine. In fact, sometimes, no matter how personal the ceremony, standard vows are a great choice—which I learned in 2017 during what I refer to as my personal Super Bowl of Weddings. (Halftime show: Adele hummed the "Bridal March.")

The bride and groom were both professional writers, so I was intimidated to write a ceremony for them and flattered beyond belief that they'd asked me to. It was wonderful working for this couple. The ceremony and entire wedding night were loaded with personal touches. I also MC'd the reception, so I got to participate in the whole event, (and witness the funniest best man speech EVER). It was a dream gig, and I have never been so sad when a wedding was over.

The ceremony was intensely personal, but the couple decided to repeat often-used vows. This was unusual for me on two counts: one,

I do not like doing the repeat-after-me thing for vows—I feel like I should be separate from this section unless I am doing The Asking, and with that choice, I am asking questions, and nobody is repeating anything. Two, the vows they were repeating were very traditional vows. Here's the thing: this was the perfect choice for them. This was their way of acknowledging the gravitas of the occasion by having something universally recognizable to anchor the personal touches surrounding it. And they *still* found a way to personalize it by adding exactly one killer line.

 Here's what we had in place for their vows: "I, [Groom] / take thee, [Bride] / to be my wedded wife / to have and to hold / from this day forward / for better, for worse / for richer, for poorer / in sickness and in health / to love and to cherish / till death do us part..."

And here is the one line they added that brought the whole thing back to them: "...and also as ghosts / just in case that's a thing."

That last bit about the ghosts, plus the colloquial "in case that's a thing," planted them in their generation, alluded to the humorous and unknowable prospect of life as ghosts (no matter what Ebenezer Scrooge, Hamlet, or Casper say), and kept within an established serious linguistic rhythm.

I love that couple so much. I loved this line, so I stole it, and now I'm giving it to you. You're welcome.

The Asking

Some couples do not want to speak out loud, at their wedding or anywhere, any more than they absolutely have to. For these people, we do The Asking.

The Asking sounds like a horror film about a little girl cursed to murder every person who asks her what her name is, featuring a tortured Liam Neeson as her dad, a tortured Nicole Kidman as her mom, and a world-weary Morgan Freeman as an exhausted town priest. But The Asking is actually just the officiant/celebrant/imam/priest/rabbi asking a series of questions to which the couple answers, individually, "I do."

The questions asked represent the vows and intentions that the couple does not want to say out loud. So, these questions need to be mostly serious, though the pattern can be mixed up with specific and humorous questions. As long as there are more serious questions than humorous questions, it'll be fine. A teaspoon of humor helps the gravitas go down (*Marry* Poppins). I give an example of a good balance of questions in Sample Ceremony: Kathryn and Iggy on page 118.

This is also a great opportunity to involve the guests, to ask them questions which will allow them to publicly vow their support for the couple. The officiant can ask the guests if they support the couple. The guests will yell "We do!" as loud as they can. Here's the thing about groups of people: people will yell out loud with no inhibitions if they know that everyone else is yelling the same thing at the same time. (This is why it's easy for even the shiest wallflower to yell "Let's go Red Sox!!!" in unison with a hundred other die-hard Red Sox fans at Yankee Stadium. If they yelled alone, they'd be taken out to Monument Park and buried alive.) Involving the guests is a great way to get them to participate, to remind them that they are part of a live event, that they can have an effect on the proceedings, and that they are not just watching something on TV.

It's fine to do combinations of all these things. It is very common for couples to say their own personal vows, then answer a series of "I do" questions. Some choose this just because they love the idea of saying "I do" (It's so wedding-y!). Couples can even combine alternate narrative approaches and ask *themselves* questions (best when done by imitating Cher's accent in *Moonstruck*):

- Do I choose to love you each and every day, to the best of my ability, as one nation, under God, for the land of the free and the home of the brave? I do.
- Do I promise to be your lawfully wedded wife today, tomorrow, all through next week, forever, and on holidays? As a matter of fact, I do.
- Do I promise to keep the details of my paleo diet to myself? That's a great question; I'm glad I asked it. Now that I mention it, I do.

Couples can devise a series of questions to ask each other, and have their partner answer the questions:

- Do you promise to support my love of wildlife no matter where in the world this passion of mine takes us?
- *I do.*
- Do you promise to try to quit drinking coffee with me for two days every five years?
- *I do.*
- Do you promise to continue doing that thing you do for me every Thursday? You know the one.
- *I do. And, I do.*

I don't get that last one.
Don't worry about it. It's an oblique *Family Guy* reference, and I'm not going to explain it because you're too pure.

Blended Families

If *The Brady Bunch* taught us nothing else, it taught us that sometimes people who are getting married or remarried have children from previous relationships. No other part of a wedding ceremony is more deserving of personalized recognition than when the couple acknowledges their responsibilities to the children who will now refer to them as their stepmom or stepdad.

The gesture need not be belabored, but it is worth mentioning, at the very least. Marriages are a blending of two families into one and children make this immediately apparent. These human beings, who will be affected by the new marriage as much (or almost as much) as the couple themselves, heighten the magnitude of the decision to become married. All weddings should illustrate the importance of blending a family through their ceremonies. When the mighty rhetoric of fidelity, trust, hard work, communication, love, sensitivity, reliability, selflessness, and unity is cast not just upon the starry-eyed couple, but upon them *and* the innocent eyes of their children, the full reality of the event is much more powerful—like experiencing fireworks in person instead of on TV.

In some ceremonies I've officiated for blended families, the couple made vows to the children as well as their new spouse. The children have stood with the couple, for all to see, embodying the seriousness of joining together forever. Even one child on each side can make the ceremony seem a part of something much bigger. The children in these weddings are living symbols of unity unto themselves.

Beyond acknowledging the children with vows, it can be symbolic to offer them a gift. The gift can be a key, symbolizing that wherever the children go to stay, they are home. It can be a necklace containing a version of the wedding band; it can be some kind of framed promissory document for the children to display in their room, a reminder of the seriousness with which the new spouse is approaching their role as stepdad or stepmom.

Just as couples should commit to their decision to get married long before the wedding day, couples with blended families should prepare their kids for this momentous change in their lives well before the ceremony. The pomp and circumstance of a wedding is an opportunity to make the adjustment real, but it is better to ease the kids into this transformation every single day, for a significant stretch of time before the wedding, to lessen the shock of the wedding day's transformative transitional effect. In other words, the blending of a family should begin way before the wedding, not *at* the wedding.

Ultimately, wedding ceremonies are guided by love. A ceremony designed with love, to showcase love, to explain love, to celebrate love, to delight in love and give thanks for love will have a loving effect on anyone lucky enough to observe or be a part of it—including the children.

CHAPTER 9

. . .

Exchange of Jewelry and Other Rituals

♡ ⧉ ∞ 🕯

If the emotionally vulnerable parents, bridal party members, and guests aren't crying yet, they should be by the time the ring exchange is over.

The Ring Exchange

The most iconic symbols of weddings (other than $$$$$) are the wedding rings, the pieces of jewelry that will remind you of your wedding day every day and also send a clear sign to any stranger hitting on you at a bar that you are morally no longer available.

If you are open to sharing, you can include details about how the rings were made, or where you bought the rings, or to whom the rings used to belong, or make up phrases that might be inscribed on the inside of the rings. (*I'm forever yours . . . faithfully*; *I-eee-I will always love you-ooooo*; *Put it back on.*) I married a couple who forged their rings themselves at a class in Italy. That was a pretty cool detail, so we mentioned it. It took no time at all, and we moved right on to the ring exchange language.

When you exchange wedding rings, you go one at a time, placing the ring onto the tip of your partner's ring finger while repeating short phrases after the celebrant. While this is the most poignant ceremonial moment of every wedding, it provides a prime opportunity for razzle-dazzle surprise. Remember, any jolt out of a pattern brings surprise. I am not saying that you *should* place a surprise moment in this section, I am just saying that you *can*. And that you *should*.

The wedding band is usually a simple piece of round metal, nothing as elaborate as the engagement ring. It is possible to make something of the ring exchange moment in a way that does not slow down the proceedings: at this point, the love snowball should be rolling downhill, picking up speed to create an avalanche of emotion. One strategically placed banana peel will have little effect on the avalanche.

For example, the short phrases you repeat will fall into a very serious repeat-after-me-pattern. Break the pattern with something inane. For example, I test my couples' sense of humor with exactly one line:

after the groom goes through the entire process of giving the bride her ring, repeating my serious phrases and sliding the ring securely onto her finger, and the bride is now going through the same process, and we all expect her to say the same things he just did. To trip up the pattern, I have her begin to say the same kind of thing he did, but then I have her say, in a sweet, upbeat voice, *"Thank you for my beautiful ring."*

This gets guests laughing every single blessed time we do this. I think this line works because the bride is simply being polite; the guy just gave her a ring, and she is saying thank you, the way you do when anybody gives you something you like. So, it is a truthful moment that nobody expects. I've found that people also appreciate the opportunity to laugh in the middle of ugly-crying; it feels good.

Right after that line, I return to the serious repeat-after-me rhythm, which the ear falls right back into since this is what feels right; consequently, the seriousness of the moment is restored. The banana peel does not impede the avalanche.

I know this is a small thing, but since I know it works, I suggest it. This is just one idea. Feel free to throw in any momentum-jarring line you like. (*Gosh, this is getting real.*) (*I've been looking forward to this moment my whole life.*) (*This is more exciting than the time we stole that Camaro.*)

Wearing the Rings

There are different philosophies regarding on which finger to place the wedding band and what to do with the engagement ring during a ceremony. When a couple exchanges wedding bands during the ceremony, ideally, the ring finger is bare so that the wedding band, once on the finger, can live closest to the person's heart. So, if one or both members of the couple are wearing an engagement ring, I ask them to temporarily wear their engagement ring on a different finger, for the ceremony only. Usually, they just switch the engagement ring over to their right hand (on whichever finger it will fit), then put the engagement ring back on their left ring finger after the ceremony, locking in the wedding band.

Some traditions have the engagement ring switched permanently to the third finger of the left hand, but this is often problematic considering how much bigger our "I am displeased with you" fingers are compared to our ring fingers. In some countries, it is common tradition to wear the wedding rings on the fourth finger of the right hand. Why? Because some countries just insist on being different. Some same-sex couples wear their rings on their right hands, as a way to distinguish their monogamous relationship and/or marriage outside heterosexual norms, whether they are legally married or simply committed to each other.

Sometimes the engagement ring doesn't fit on any other finger. In these cases, I assure the couple that they can just switch the ring order on their finger after the ceremony. It is not a crucial detail—in that it won't stop the wedding or mean they aren't married—but it is a symbolic and meaningful one.

Ultimately, I encourage couples to do whatever they would like to with their rings. Their rings, their ceremony, and their marriage are unique to them. There is no official, secret language of rings, in which the choice of ring finger communicates an agreed-upon set of signals. I wear my wedding band on my left ring finger, but mostly because I've gained some weight since I got married and that sucker is on there tight.

Okay, so the rings are on the fingers, and the ceremony is pretty much done. But wait! There could be more!

Other Rituals

Unity Rituals

If couples want to include a unity ritual in their ceremony, this is where I tend to place it in the ceremony (see also Wedopedia: Rituals). The various props of unity rituals, such as jars of sand, candles, rope, or memory boxes, are usually waiting upon a tastefully decorated table upstage center, directly behind where I have been speaking. I step aside to reveal the table and its props, taking the mic stand along with me, so it does not block the guests' view. The couple steps to either side of the table, giving focus to the table's unity items. Then I narrate the meaning and steps of the ritual while the couple goes through the mechanics. Once the ritual is completed, the couple can return front and center while I often stay to the side, ceding center stage entirely to the couple.

And that's it, ceremony over, nothing left to do but pronounce them married. But wait! There could still be more!

Cultural or Religious Rituals

This part of the ceremony is also the most apt for including any other cultural or religious elements—which is not to say that there are no other parts of the ceremony where we can include such things. When I have couples whose families speak more than one language or come from a different culture, I make a point of using their language as early as the welcome section. I may intersperse linguistic or cultural details throughout the love story, wherever I deem it appropriate, useful, or opportunistic. In deciding when and how to incorporate cultural and religious elements, it's important to determine if these elements define the couple or if they are merely peripheral details from their heritage. In other words, are they asking to acknowledge these elements of culture and religion because they really believe in them, or are they merely acknowledging these elements out of an obligation to be respectful of their elders?

Solving this kind of conundrum is what separates the professionals from the amateurs. When certified Life-Cycle Celebrants are training, they spend months acquainting themselves with traditions, rituals, international cultural norms, ways to blend families of differing religious beliefs, ways to acknowledge the cornucopia of symbols and meaning that makes up our world; a dissertation on belief-blending and custom-blending opportunities could fill an entire book. And the learning never stops: every new couple offers me a reason to research something new, to find the facts and details that will contribute to a personal love story. Every experience informs the next. Every new combination presents new opportunities.

Once the couple state their intentions and are both wearing wedding rings in front of me and all the important people in their lives, in my mind they are married, no matter what cultural or religious elements we acknowledge or what bureaucratic stuff still needs to happen at City Hall. At that point, I feel what Friar Laurence was *hoping* to feel by marrying Juliet and Romeo in *Romeo & Juliet*. (He never made it happen, thanks to misunderstandings, death, and iambic pentameter. Friar Laurence was hoping to put an end to the Capulet/Montague feud by marrying Romeo and Juliet, which means he and I had the same philosophy on the potential of marriages to influence peace and ultimately save the world, which means that great minds think alike, which means that Shakespeare— or Marlowe, we'll never know—had a great mind.)

A while back, I filmed an audition video for the travel show *Globe Trekker*. My idea was to become one of their travelers, attending weddings around the world to educate viewers on the multitude of ways humans celebrate wedding unions. Still waiting to hear back from them. I maintain that it would be a great show! I'm sure they'll call any minute now. Yep. Any minute.

♥

ACT V

CHAPTER 10

· · ·

Wedding Zen

♡ ♡ 🕊 🔔

By this point in the ceremony, the guests should be eating out of the officiant's hand. (Not literally, that would be gross.) By now the guests should be engrossed in the story, crying at how beautiful it is, and paying close attention because they have no idea what will happen or what will be uttered next. Once the guests are transfixed (Happynotized!©), it's time to get real.

It's important to slow things down so everyone can grasp the importance and beauty of what they are witnessing. A party lurks just around the next few turns of phrase; this is one last opportunity to crank up the anticipation to squealing-burst levels. This moment is critical for balancing unique elements with meaning (like PBS).

When people think about their wedding ceremony, it is in the vaguest terms: they don't want it to be too long. They don't want it to be too serious. They don't want it to be frivolous, but they don't want it to go on and on either. By this point in the ceremony, whether couples have employed only a few ideas from this book or if they've taken it to heart and added creative flourishes to multiple segments of the wedding ceremony and wedding day, then this is the time to win over doubters, to assuage concerned parents, to keep the entire day genuine.

Zen is a mysterious term, one that connotes what Westerners call Eastern teachings and what Easterners just call teachings. Zen conjures images of gentle streams, a pile of stones impossibly balanced, the tranquility of green leaves, tubes of massage lotion, fresh air, quiet, solitude, manicured gardens, mountain breezes, immobile monks, or in extreme cases, immobile monks in quiet gardens next to gentle streams surrounded by impossibly balanced stones. (Mick Jagger in a headstand atop Charlie Watts.) Wedding Zen is an attitude, a return to calm, a state of relaxation, and harmony within a wedding venue. (I should trademark the phrase "Wedding Zen," then accept money every time someone uses this phrase, then give that money to charity.)

Wedding days are the opposite of Zen (zany): they are busy, complicated, distracting, detail-crazed, hopeful, nerve-wracking, exciting, burdened by unusual clothing, sloppy runners, wildflowers, wild flower girls, and a bunch of people who are about to become in-laws. Wedding days are espresso; Zen is herbal tea.

I like to carve out Wedding Zen for the couple near the end of the ceremony. Within the Zen, I like to imply that we do not have to rush, that the moment we are in is the only moment that matters, that the details of this once-in-a-lifetime experience (twice, tops) are full and clear and memorable. To do this, I slow things down and get as holistic and spiritual as I can ever be accused of getting. I get everyone to focus on what is. No more, no less.

To this point, the ceremony has had great storytelling, humor, theatrical elements that play on visual gags and make use of the space, and beautiful, true sentiments about the couple that resonate with everyone present. By this point, the guests' heartstrings have been pulled in multiple directions and now is the time to let them be whatever and wherever they may be being.

Here is what I do to invoke Wedding Zen:

I have couples notice the feeling of each other's hands, the new feeling of having those rings on their fingers.

If it is an indoor ceremony, I direct their attention to the temperature of the room, how perfect and comfortable it is.

If they decided to risk the entire ceremony on the whims of Mother Nature without an indoor or at least sheltered Plan B, I draw their attention to the raindrops, the pummeling wind, the snow, the blazing heat, the humidity . . .

I turn their attention to every single sound they hear including their cousin's baby crying, the snapping of their photographer's camera, the buzz of cicadas, the air-conditioning, the birds chirping, the mosquitoes buzzing. I keep it real: this is the time to let whatever is in everyone's mind be in everyone's mind. If we hear a helicopter, I acknowledge the helicopter. If we hear seagulls, I acknowledge the seagulls. If I hear a fire alarm because someone knocked over one of those standing candle-vase things, I mention the fire alarm. These are details couples will remember. I note every obvious sound—there will only be a few, so it won't take long.

I note what they see: the person they love more than anyone standing in front of them, the friends and family they love seated before them. I remind them that all these people have traveled from so far away to be with them because they love them, and support them, and wish only the best for them, forever. I note how happy that these details should make them feel. I invite them to hold on to this feeling in their hearts and minds forever.

It would be easy, almost too easy, to plant a surprise line here, to puncture the moment with a punch line about the guests being here to enjoy free booze, or about the bride's parents sensing money flying out of their wallets. It would be SO EASY, but I don't recommend it.

And then—my favorite moment in the entire ceremony, the moment that I look forward to more than any other moment the whole night (other than my first cocktail hour beer): I have the couple think back, if they can, to the very moment they met.

Ahhh! (Anybody have a tissue?) It's such a great moment, a moment that bridges the absolute beginning of their relationship with the current moment. In a flash, they can glimpse themselves as who they were then and who they are now.

When they've had a few seconds to think about that, and I've seen the acknowledgment of that distant moment in their eyes . . .

. . . *it's time to marry the golly gee heck out of them!!!!!*

Golly gee heck?
I don't want to alienate any of my readers with profanity.

CHAPTER 11

...

Pronouncement and Kiss

♡ 💕 🍾 🎺

This is the moment in the ceremony where we launch the party.

This is the moment when all the bartenders, servers, cooks, and staff take a deep breath, readying for the onslaught. Prayers are uttered. Discreet shots of Jaeger are downed. Rosaries are worried.

If you've followed the ideas from the ten chapters before this, you should be looking at a two-inch tap-in for Eagle. If that metaphor does nothing for you, try this instead: you should be looking at hundreds of balloons about to release on your say-so. This is a BIG MOMENT.

And yet as big a moment as this is, my advice is simply to just get to it. This is not the time to delay the happiness poised to erupt. The couple is excited, the guests are excited, the ceremony has been entertaining and meaningful, everyone in the room wants the couple to be married just as much as the couple does and everyone is ready to cheer. To delay this moment further would be like your grandfather launching into an anecdote about his youth right before you're ready to pull out of his driveway and head back to the hotel after a long, politically adversarial Thanksgiving Day. Delaying here would be like the opening act at a concert doing one last song after the song they'd said was going to be their last song. The longer this part is delayed, the lower the guests' estimation of the ceremony will be; finish it. We've filled the glass to the brim—any more vodka in there will just spill to the floor. The elevator is full; if one more person gets on, the doors won't be able to close. We've won our Oscar, thanked everyone in our family, and the musicians are playing us off. We've filled the back seat with thirty clowns, loaded the musket with shot, pumped up the T-shirt gun, pulled the pin from the grenade, withdrawn from—okay I think you get the idea.

Pronunciation of Marriage (MARE•idge)

Here's the most official-sounding thing to be uttered during the ceremony. Every ceremonialist around the world should have fun with this part, to make it unique to them.

By the powers vested in me by the Super-Duper State of New York...

... by the corn-growing hub that is Nebraska...

... by the hockey-mad State of Minnesota...

... by the undrained swamp of DC...

... by the insurance gurus of Connecticut...

... by the suntanned illuminati of California...

I hereby declare you husband and wife [married/spouses/partners in life]. You may kiss [the bride/each other/in public/like teenagers under the bleachers].

Note to whoever is doing the ceremony—get the heck out of the way so you are not in the kiss photos!

Presentation of the Newly Married Couple

Old-school couples will request that they be presented as "Mr. and Mrs. So-and-So" before they recess down the aisle. It's another surefire applause line, and yet it can be re-imagined to be even more fun. This is a moment where any interesting, unique, funny details can be linked to the moment.

- Ladies and gentlemen, I present to you the most generous tippers this side of Madison Avenue.
- Ladies and gentleman, I present to you the most recently married people in this room.
- Ladies and gentlemen, I present to you the most romantic pair of left-handed black-jack dealers I've ever met.

CHAPTER 12

...

Recessional

Music and mess-making! It's time for a moment so fun, even bald people let their hair down!

Recessional music should be alive, recognizable, and joyous. My favorite recessional, other than the dance party wedding where hundreds of balloons were released, was one where an undercover chorus arose from among the guests and sang beautiful gospel music that had everyone in a good mood. The chorus then formed an alley of their own, to serenade guests as they left the ceremonial area and headed to cocktail hour.

The music should be loud because people will be cheering; if the music is loud, the cheers will get louder.

Then it's time to get that parade out of the ceremonial space.

The Couple

The couple has their dramatic, joyous kiss, lingers in the warm safety of each other's embrace, kisses a few more times, retrieves a bouquet if necessary, then links arms and recesses to thunderous applause.

To make the photos even more exciting, it's always a great idea to fill the air with rose petals, confetti, rice, ribbons, (couscous, string cheese, bologna), or bubbles as everyone recesses down the aisle, or whatever walkway you've invented. People love throwing things at other people.

It's fun to form human gauntlets for the couple to pass under by having people from both sides of the aisle hold their hands above their heads and join fingertips with people across the aisle. Alternatively, an archway of palm fronds would be scenic. The Navy and Marine Corps make an Arch of Swords for the couple to pass through. (The Army makes an Arch of Sabers.) A limbo stick would be really fun, especially for a beach wedding. No matter what you would like to have happen among these options, your officiant should announce this request and explain the idea so guests are ready to take part: "You should have a little container of confetti at your seat; get that confetti ready, and when the couple walks down the aisle just forty-five seconds from now, pelt 'em with it!!!"

I think it would be great fun if the couple could recess by leaping off a stage of some sort and crowd-surfing like rock stars.

Best Man and Maid/Matron of Honor

Usually, these two are the closest to the middle—they link arms and recess. No need to do anything special, just get out of there. At this point in the ceremony, we are in the divine stage of "leave 'em wanting more."

Bridesmaids and Groomsmen, Two by Two or As Needed

At this point, the bridesmaids and groomsmen from each side can pair up or triple up as needed in the middle, then recess. Sometimes, if the flower girls and ring bearers are old enough and game for it, you can make some fun recessing combos out of them and the Bs and Gs. Mix up the pairings. Tall groomsman/short flower girl? Love it. Little ring bearer with two gorgeous bridesmaids? Photo gold!!!

The idea of the recessional is to get everyone out of the ceremonial area, which is often also the reception area, so the staff can flip the room. Still, I am in favor of the recessional being dance-intensive, with everyone either free-styling it to some great music we all love ("Crazy Little Thing Called Love" by Queen, "Beautiful Day" by U2, "Let's Go Crazy" by Prince, "Happy" by Pharrell Davis, "Dancing Queen" by ABBA), or having the bridal party exit with some minor, manageable choreography. Theatrically, this should be a parade of joy, a group of Party Pied-Pipers leading the way to cocktail hour.

I attended a taping of *The Late Show with Stephen Colbert* once. During commercial breaks, Jean Batiste and his band, Stay Human, would wander, in a row, up and down the aisles in what he calls a "Love Riot." They would keep playing and grooving as they walked, and it just made you want to join in and follow them wherever they would go.

We didn't, of course, because we were supposed to stick around to find out what the next guest was up to. (It was David Schwimmer; I haven't seen him since.) If you have musicians who can walk with their instruments, this would be a fun way to guide the bridal party and guests to the cocktail hour.

And who can forget the scene in *Love, Actually* when the band arose from among the guests at Kiera Knightley's character's wedding early in the movie to play "All You Need is Love"? What's that? You did forget that scene? Oh. Well, yeah, this happened. It was Cute, Actually.

And this marks the end of the ceremony. Twenty to twenty-five minutes after it began, it's over, done, kaput, finito. The cocktail hour is just beginning. The guests should be abuzz with what they just witnessed. Everybody loves you for taking the time to work with the person performing your ceremony to make it unique.

Congratulations! You did it!

Now, go be married people.

SAMPLE CEREMONIES

So what does a unique ceremony look like? I've included two samples in this section to give you an idea.

The first wedding (Kathryn and Iggy—fictional!) is the kind of wedding I do all the time. It takes place in a non-religious venue, an actual former monastery in Cincinnati that has been repurposed for all kinds of events, including weddings. The sample includes a couple that comes from different cultures and religious beliefs, although they are both American. It contains both serious tones and humorous tones, striking a balance to create a ceremony that is both delightful and meaningful. In each sample, you can get an idea of different stage directions to consider. You can see the order of events laid out, get a feeling for the stage mechanics of a ceremony, and get a sense for how a twenty-minute ceremony looks on the page. These samples should give you an idea of how to linger on aspects of a love story in some parts while moving it along in other parts; to include elements of surprise to hook your listeners. You can see how the Love Story anchors the entire ceremony by celebrating the couple's story with honesty and passion. I've included some notes to show you what my intention is in certain sections, to show you how methods I've outlined in the book can be used in practice.

The purpose of the second sample wedding (Ben and Natalya—also fictional!) is to show what an outside-the-box, over-the-top wedding ceremony can look like. Just imagine how nutty the actual love story for this one could be! (I totally wrote a love story for these fictional people, but I withheld it because it might distract you from all the staging.) The second sample wedding is meant to unscrew the lid of the possibility jar.

Atmosphere

MUSIC CUE: A string trio plays '80s and '90s hits as guests arrive, mingle, and compare outfits . . . ♡

Once the celebrant and venue coordinator and wedding planner have communicated that the guests are seated and ready, the bridal party is lined up and ready, and the photographers, video people, and musicians are all ready to begin . . . Celebrant Christopher Shelley enters.

MUSIC CUE: Upon seeing Chris begin to enter, our string trio switches to an upbeat version of "Losing My Religion" by R.E.M. ✪ *Celebrant dances up the aisle, then through a row full of guests a la Ellen DeGeneres, taking a moment to dance with one or more guests, then all the way to the ceremonial area . . . 🎸*

MUSIC CUE: "Losing My Religion" fades out as Chris speaks . . .

♡   Non-traditional music of the bride and groom's generation!

✪   Irony! I'm non-denominational! And I love Michael Stipe.

🎸   Establishing the moment guests see me that this ceremony will be different.

Introduction♡

CELEBRANT: Good evening, everybody. Congratulations on making the guest list. My name is Christopher Shelley and I love my job. I am a wedding officiant and celebrant, which means that my job is to marry our bride and groom to each other and to celebrate why they are getting married.

Tonight is an opportunity for all of you to connect with people you haven't seen for a while or whom you're meeting for the first time. You have a wonderful night ahead of you.

Welcome to Ohio, welcome to Cincinnati, welcome to the Monastery Event Center, and welcome to the wedding of Kathryn and Iggy.🐝

Thank you for your enthusiasm. Our string trio is ready to play some more beautiful music, the wedding party is ready to make their big dramatic entrance, and I've had lots of caffeine.🗝 Ladies and gentleman, I hereby declare the wedding planning to be officially over! Let the ceremony begin.

Processional

MUSIC CUE: String trio plays pretty version of The Cure's "Just Like Heaven."💎

♡   Forty-five seconds to establish my personality and style with the guests, to get them in a good mood—I am my own warm-up act!

🐝   Remember, this is a fictional wedding; in a real wedding, I would say their last names too.

🗝   Planted words "enthusiasm" and "party" for obvious reasons, and "caffeine" for guests to subconsciously associate caffeine/being awake.

💎   Recognizable, fitting of bride and groom, different than expected/ normal wedding music.

Groom Iggy enters with his parents, Musa and Karen. Iggy kisses Mom on the cheek and hugs her; Iggy and his Dad hug, then Iggy's parents sit. Iggy stands STAGE LEFT/downstage of Celebrant.

Best Man Charles enters, doing his best supermodel/Zoolander walk up the aisle, has a complicated and obviously oft-practiced handshake combo with Iggy, then takes his spot STAGE LEFT of Iggy.

Groomsman Tim and Bridesmaid Joanne enter, doing a simple part-nered waltz; at the top of the aisle Tim kisses Joanne's hand, then Joanne establishes the end of the row far STAGE RIGHT while Tim goes STAGE LEFT of Best Man.

Groomsman Will and Bridesmaid Elvira enter, tossing confetti at the guests,♡at the top of the aisle, Will goes to kiss Elvira's hand but ends up kissing his own, then they take their places STAGE LEFT/STAGE RIGHT, Elvira filling closer to the middle (STAGE LEFT of Joanne).

Groomsman Anthony and Bridesmaid Selma enter, tossing packets of tissues to each row of guests;♋at the top of the aisle, they toss each other a packet, then take their spots STAGE LEFT/STAGE RIGHT.

Maid of Honor Francine enters, wearing a sash that reads, "I Need a Drink."

Ring Bearers Justin (8) and Ravi (9) enter on skateboards; they take their seats with their parents in the front row.🛹

Flower Girls Gabby (5) and Sarah (6) enter, tossing little individual open bags of flower petals straight into the air above them, so when they open, flower petals trickle down slowly.💎They continue this all the way up the aisle, then take their seats with their parents or legal guardians in the first row.

CELEBRANT: Please stand to greet the bride.
Guests stand.

♡　　Visually unexpected and photo-worthy.

♋　　Practical and unexpected.

🛹　　Fits the kids' personalities, and the speed of their entrance is unexpected!

💎　　Visually more interesting than the usual flower-to-the floor dropping they usually do, photo worthy.

MUSIC CUE: "Just Like Heaven" winds down...dramatic pause... really dramatic, like, long enough to make the groom wonder if the bride is showing up...then the Bride's song begins: "Only You" by Yaz (or Yazoo, as they are known in Europe).

Bride Kathryn enters, looking spectacular, escorted by her father, Jim, and her mother, Doris. Mom and Dad bring Kathryn just past the first row of seats, where they pause. Dad lifts Kathryn's veil to unveil her face. Mom/Dad/Daughter have a moment (kiss/hug etc.).

Groom Iggy steps forward, kisses Kathryn's mom on the cheek, shakes Kathryn's dad's hand.

Iggy's parents stand again, the men shake hands, the women kiss each other's cheeks, then the men kiss the women's cheeks.

All four parents, Iggy and Kathryn stand in a circle, their hands in the middle of the circle—all of their hands on top of Iggy/Kathryn's, like a team before a game. One by one, the four parents remove their hand from the other hands... until the only two people holding hands are Iggy and Kathryn.

Iggy escorts Kathryn to the ceremonial matrimonial sweet spot where Chris is waiting. All four parents take their seats

CELEBRANT: You may be seated, thank you.

Guests sit.

MOH arranges Kathryn's dress.

MUSIC CUE: The music comes to a graceful stop.

ALL GROOMSMEN, BRIDESMAIDS, BEST MAN, MAN OF HONOR, CHRIS, to Iggy/Kathryn: **WELCOME TO YOUR WEDDING!!!**

Guests cheer.

ALL BRIDAL PARTY: **WHO DEY? WHO DEY? WHO DEY THINK GONNA MARRY KATHRYN?**

Guests laugh at reference to this cheer that Cincinnati Bengals fans yell at games.♡

♡   Always better to incorporate the bridal party because they really serve no purpose whatsoever otherwise.

Welcome

CELEBRANT: Welcome everybody. We are happy that so many of you could make it here today. It is very important to celebrate these happy transitions in our lives. One of my favorite things about weddings is learning how far people are willing to travel to be here. We have honored friends and family here from ALL OVER THE WORLD, including Kentucky♡... also Florida, Connecticut, Maine, Virginia, New York, and, of course, Ohio. We also have guests here from as far away as France and Iran. Welcome! *Bienvenue* and *Khosh amadid*! ☜

Thanks

CELEBRANT: Kathryn and Iggy are so grateful to all of you for being here tonight. They have been so excited for their wedding and they've been longing to share their happiness with you, the people who matter to them most. If you are in this room right now, it means that you are very important to them. Or that you work for the Monastery Event Center, in which case you are still very important to us.

Honor Parents

CELEBRANT: Iggy and Kathryn are especially happy to have their parents here today. Musa and Karen have been married for twenty-five years and, not that it's a competition or anything, Jim and Doris have been married for thirty-three years. You are an inspiration to all of us. You are proof that long-lasting love is possible, and that listening to your wife really works. ☜

♡   Contrast of world/Kentucky. Pause makes it seem like Kentucky is all there is.

☜   Polite to include a moment of foreign language.

☜   Take a moment for parents.

Love Story

CELEBRANT: Tonight we'll celebrate Iggy and Kathryn. We'll celebrate the factors that brought them together and keep them together. We'll find out how a woman who lived in New York and a man who lived in New York found each other . . . in New York. We'll find out how Iggy proposed and whether Kathryn said yes. *This is their love story.*♡

Three years ago, Iggy and Kathryn were busy being good people. Both were in New York, at a fundraiser for the Red Cross.♋ They didn't go to find love, they went to enjoy free drinks and cubed cheese. But when mutual friends introduced them, they began talking and continued talking. After hours had gone by, they looked up to see that Kathryn's Credit Suisse friends and Iggy's Goldman Sachs friends had all abandoned them. And that was fine with them. They felt comfortable together, and they felt as if they'd begun a conversation that could last a lifetime.

Their first date began with a walk along the High Line, which Kathryn mentioned reminded her of Cincinnati. Iggy had never heard anyone say that something in New York reminded them of Cincinnati. A rainstorm forced their date into an art gallery, and then to the restaurant closest to the art gallery. They had an incredible dinner, then later, just as her cab was pulling up, they had a magical first kiss. It was so good, they had to shoo the cab driver away only to discover that must have been the last available cab in Manhattan that rainy night. Iggy walked her home, like a gentleman, and after they said goodnight they had the most ridiculous hop in their step.🎻

They took very different paths toward each other. Iggy is half-Iranian, half-American. His dad was a lapsed Muslim, an Iranian small

---

♡   Opening inspired by Stephen Colbert's opening sequence on his old show, *The Colbert Report*, because it builds up the excitement of discovery in a tongue-in-cheek way.

♋   Paints the picture of how their lives crossed paths while simultaneously revealing character.

🎻   220 words for their entire first date—broad brush strokes.

businessman, and his mom was a lapsed Catholic, a vociferous academic at New York University. Like the Monastery Event Center itself, they used to be religious but now cater to anyone who will pay them.♡ Iggy had spent his life as American as can be, the blend of cultures and beliefs in his family enriching him, his parents making sure that he was aware of his heritage but allowing him to make up his own mind about his beliefs and identity.

Kathryn grew up as American as can be, with parents who couldn't be more American, out in Cincinnati, Ohio. Her dad was a hard-working cop and her Mom was an even harder-working nurse, but they made plenty of time for their daughter. They raised her Christian, taught her to be a good person, supported her enthusiasms, taught her how to shoot a gun, always stayed involved in her school work, and were present for every crisis and achievement.

Iggy and Kathryn loved examining their families' differences, marveling that no matter what kind of families they came from, their families would be interesting to them, and it wouldn't make a lick of a difference in how crazy in love they were with each other.♋

It wasn't always easy. Nothing worth anything is ever easy.🎻 Just as they were getting closer, distance became an issue. Iggy's firm wanted him to work in the Paris office. He had to take the offer. When he told Kathryn, she cried, and then he cried. They both took turns face-down on his couch, crying.

They made it work.♦ It's easier these days with email and Skype and Facetime and WhatsApp—but that didn't make them like it. They saw each other as often as they could, Kathryn making the huge sacrifice of having to spend time in Paris to be with him. During her first visit, Iggy took her on a romantic boat ride on the Seine, and they told each other

---

♡ Always good to make a smart reference about the surroundings.

♋ These last three paragraphs show how people from different cultures and upbringings can be points of fascination and not fear.

🎻 Storytelling 101: Give the heroes obstacles.

♦ Overcoming the obstacles!

"I love you" for the first time. They traveled all over: Barcelona, Bruges, Vienna, Prague, Budapest, London, Berlin, and one very long weekend at the Sound of Music festival in Salzburg. They ate interesting food, they talked to people of all different cultures and religions, they navigated train stations and airports and country roads and learned so much about each other as they did so.♡

One Christmas, Iggy flew to Cincinnati to see her and to meet her parents for the first time. Kathryn's parents had never seen an Iranian before, and they were shocked at how normal his American accent was.

But that's America for you: once you meet a person from a different culture, whether it's an Ohioan meeting a New Yorker, an American meeting an Iranian or in this case both, once you actually spend time with a person you realize that we're all just humans. Love is the same everywhere. Iggy made multiple visits to Cincinnati, despite the long flights, strategically gaining her parents' trust. During one visit, he did the traditional thing: he asked her father for permission to marry Kathryn. And her dad said, "Hell no."♡♡

It wasn't that he didn't like Iggy. He did like him, even though Iggy knew nothing about college football. Her dad knew that Kathryn didn't like having a boyfriend in Paris.

Iggy promised he'd do the right thing—and on that condition, Kathryn's dad gave his blessing.

The next time Iggy and Kathryn visited Cincinnati, Iggy treated her family to a riverboat ride on the Ohio River, because when you work at Goldman Sachs, it's what you do. Despite living in Ohio their entire lives, neither she nor her parents had ever done one of these rides, so it was a first for all of them. And that wasn't the end of firsts.🎸

♡   A montage of images, making a whirlwind romance accessible in the guests' minds.

♡♡   Storytelling left-turn: Dad saying no is unexpected.

🎸   Transition!

At one point, Iggy pulled Kathryn aside, and they leaned against a railing. Iggy said, "I have two surprises for you." ♡

He told her he'd gotten himself reassigned to the New York office. She clasped her hands to her mouth and began trembling because she had a feeling she knew what the second surprise would be.

And then Iggy said some beautiful things to Kathryn, things that only she should ever hear. He got down on one knee. He took out a gorgeous engagement ring, holding it reverently between his thumb and index finger. He asked her to marry him. Kathryn said yes, and screamed, and jumped into his arms, and he twirled her round and round. ☯

They told her family and spent the rest of the night in an alcohol-drenched selfie-fest, with the backdrop of the Cincinnati skyline.

Kathryn said yes to Iggy's proposal because she trusts him completely. She loves every minute she spends with him. She loves experiencing the world with him, and she loves how he makes her laugh no matter where they are or what's going on. She loves how thoughtful and kind he is. She loves how he loves his family and friends. She loves that she can call out all the answers on Jeopardy before he can. ✐

Iggy asked Kathryn to marry him because he can't imagine being without her. The world is full of so many things to experience and explore and he loves experiencing everything and exploring everywhere with Kathryn. He loves how selfless she is, how beautiful, how reliable she is. He loves that he can beat her at Scrabble even though she's such a smarty-pants with her Jeopardy skills. ♦

Together they are proud that they have maintained a lively friendship within their romance. It is an honor to stand up here with two

♡   Cliff-hanger! What will the surprises be? We get to experience what
     Kathryn experienced.
☯   Linking the Seine river "I love you" to the Ohio River proposal is use-
     ful for framing and perspective.
✐   Breaks up saccharine detailing of love in an unexpected way that is
     still completely true.
♦   Breaks up saccharine detailing of love in an unexpected way that is
     still completely true and echoes to previous paragraph.

126   BEST. CEREMONY. EVER.

such deserving people and to say with absolute conviction that they are getting married for all the best reasons.♡

The Asking ☙

CELEBRANT: Iggy and Kathryn, I have a few questions for you to clarify your intentions for each other today. The answer we'd all really love to hear in response to each question is "I do."

Iggy do you want to marry Kathryn? ✎

IGGY: I do.

CELEBRANT: Do you promise to be Kathryn's faithful husband, to love her every day, through every challenge, as long as you both shall live? ♦

IGGY: I do.

CELEBRANT: Do you promise to treat her as your equal and as your best friend?♡ ♡

IGGY: I do.

CELEBRANT: Do you promise to be honest with her, to listen to her, to be vulnerable with her, and to share with her your deepest thoughts and feelings? ☙☙

♡   These three paragraphs detail her love for him, his love for her, their love for what they've achieved with their relationship. It's all about love and it's all about two people creating a beautiful third thing that we call a marriage.

☙   When couples don't want to do personal vows, these questions amount to vows.

✎   Serious question

♦   Serious question

♡♡   Serious question

☙☙   Serious question

IGGY: I do.

CELEBRANT: Do you promise to be the best in-law you can be? ♡

IGGY: I do.

CELEBRANT: Kathryn, do you want to marry Iggy? ⌘

KATHRYN: I do.

CELEBRANT: Do you promise to be Iggy's faithful wife, to love him every day, through every challenge, as long as you both shall live? ⌘

KATHRYN: I do.

CELEBRANT: Do you promise to treat him as your best friend and your most cherished companion? ♛

KATHRYN: I do.

CELEBRANT: Do you promise to be honest with him, to listen to him, to be vulnerable with him, and to share with him your deepest thoughts and feelings? ♡♡

KATHRYN: I do.

CELEBRANT: Do you promise to be the best in-law you can be? ⌘⌘

KATHRYN: I do.

CELEBRANT: Honored guests, do you promise to support this couple? ⌘⌘

GUESTS: WE DO! ♛♛

♡   Real, but not-so-serious question

⌘   Serious question

⌘   Serious question

♛   Serious question

♡♡   Serious question

⌘⌘   Real, but not-so-serious question

⌘⌘   Involve the guests!

♛♛   People love yelling out loud when they know that everyone around them will also be yelling out loud.

CELEBRANT: Do you promise to encourage their dreams, to relieve them of their fears, and to offer them advice even when they don't ask for it?

GUESTS: WE DO!

Rings

CELEBRANT: Wedding rings are a symbol of commitment and love. They represent what has been and what will always be. These rings will remind Kathryn and Iggy of this day, every day.

Who has the rings?

Best Man Charles hands Kathryn's RING to Iggy.

CELEBRANT: Iggy, you will go first. Please place Kathryn's ring on the tip of her ring finger and repeat after me.

CELEBRANT/IGGY (repeating): Kathryn, / I love you. / My heart is in this ring. / I promise to be your faithful husband, / to love you in sickness and in health, / in life and beyond. / When you look at this ring, / remember that I love you always.

CELEBRANT: You may slide the ring all the way onto her finger.

He does.

CELEBRANT: Kathryn, it's your turn.

Best Man Charles hands IGGY'S RING to Celebrant, Celebrant hands it to KATHRYN.

CELEBRANT/KATHRYN (repeating): Iggy, / Thank you for my beautiful ring.♡ / I love you. / My heart is in this ring. / I promise to be your faithful wife, / to love you in sickness and in health, / in life and beyond. / When you look at this ring, / remember that I love you always.

CELEBRANT: You may place the ring all the way onto his finger.

She does.

♡   Polite, and nobody expects it

Wedding Zen

CELEBRANT: Iggy and Kathryn, your wedding day is already flying by. Many couples remember how fleeting their own wedding day was, especially the ceremony, so I encourage you, right now, to take in every detail of this moment:

The feeling of each other's hands.♡

The temperature of the room.

Every single sound you hear.

The feeling of having all these people who love you all in the same place.

Think about the happiness that you're feeling.

Let that feeling live in your heart and your mind so you will remember it forever.

Now, for pleasing symmetry, think back to the very moment you met. ☺

Pronouncement/Kiss

CELEBRANT: It has been my honor to officiate your ceremony. Now I get to say something you've been looking forward to hearing for a long time. By the powers vested in me by the Buckeye State—the wonderful State of Ohio—I now pronounce you husband and wife. You may kiss.

Chris gets out of the way, ducking STAGE LEFT with the groomsmen so he is not in the kiss photos.

Kathryn and Iggy kiss.

The guests go nuts!

♡   Improvisational—using whatever details are obvious to all of us

☺   Connects two big-bang moments of the couple's relationship, the one that began the whole thing and the one that is just about to happen . . .

Recessional

MUSIC CUE: "Beautiful Day" by U2

Kathryn retrieves her bouquet from the Maid of Honor Francine.

Kathryn and Iggy exit.

Francine and Charles exit.

Anthony and Selma exit.

Will and Elvira exit.

Tim and Joanne exit.

Chris invites first row of honored guests to exit, bride's side first, then groom's side.

Chris exits.

Kathryn and Iggy live a long, happy life together.

THE (FICTIONAL) WEDDING

OF

BEN AND NATALYA

THE (REAL) PARK PLAZA HOTEL
NEW YORK, NY

CELEBRANT: CHRISTOPHER SHELLEY
ILLUMINATING CEREMONIES

Atmosphere

MUSIC CUE: The first thing guests see and hear as they step through tall doors to enter the vast Park Plaza Hotel ceremony room is a pair of drummers on a landing, playing a subtle Caribbean beat. As guests wander down the red-carpeted steps to the seating area of the vast Park Plaza ceremony space, they are stunned by its elaborate lighting, architecture, staging, jaw-dropping floral arrangements and general iconic elegance.

Closer to ceremony time, when all the guests are seated, the drummers strap their drums around their shoulders and continue playing as they stand. They are joined by a trumpet player, a gal playing accordion, and another gal on tambourine. The five of them march down the fabled steps of the Plaza to the ceremonial area, playing their music the whole time. They take their places STAGE LEFT of the ceremony space, on their own mini-stage, and their music intensifies, crescendos, as . . .

Celebrant Christopher Shelley enters, dances down the steps, down the aisle steps, a real show.

MUSIC CUE: As Chris arrives on the stage, the jam comes down to a solitary drummer underscoring the mood . . . drummer keeps the beat just above a whisper as Chris speaks.

Introduction

CELEBRANT: [Chris introduces himself and gets the guests into a good mood.]

MUSIC CUE: A trumpet flourish!

CELEBRANT: [Chris makes them laugh.]

MUSIC CUE: A joyous riffing of all the instruments emerges, flourishes . . .

CELEBRANT: [Chris cues the processional music to begin.]

Processional

MUSIC CUE: Riffing drops off . . . the accordionist, solo, plays romantic Parisian street music . . .

Groom Ben enters with his parents, Gerald and Kathy. Halfway up the aisle, the three of them do a mock Rockettes kick line to an accordion burst of "New York, New York" as they approach the ceremonial area, then music reverts to Parisian street music. Ben has a moment with Mom and Dad (kiss/hug etc.), then they sit. Ben stands STAGE LEFT/downstage of Celebrant.

MUSIC CUE: Accordion player fades and drummers take over . . .

Best Man Chaz enters, does some bodybuilder poses at the top of the aisle, gives Ben a bear hug that lasts too long, puts him down, take his spot immediately STAGE LEFT of Ben.

Groomsman Tom and Bridesmaid Joan enter, shaking maracas and dancing; at the top of the aisle they bow to each other, then Joan takes her place STAGE RIGHT establishing the end of her row, Tom goes wide STAGE LEFT of Best Man, establishing the end of his row.

Groomsman Bill and Bridesmaid Ellie enter, blowing soap bubbles at the guests; at the top of the aisle, they create a huge double-bubble, wave at each other, then take their places, her STAGE RIGHT of Chris, him STAGE RIGHT of Tom.

Groomsman Antoine and Bridesmaid Sandra enter, doing a dramatic tango dance up the aisle, even more impressive considering the stairs, then take their places, her just STAGE LEFT of Ellie, him just STAGE RIGHT of Bill.

Groomsman Zach and Bridesmaid Heather enter, normally, at the top of the aisle they bump hips, then do a complicated handshake/fist bump routine, then take their places, her STAGE LEFT of Sandra, him just STAGE RIGHT of Antoine.

MUSIC CUE: Tambourine and trumpet joins in with the drums . . .

Maid of Honor (MOH) Margaret enters, carried on the shoulders of two huge, muscular guys in sleeveless tuxedos. The men place her in position STAGE RIGHT of Heather, then take up space at the far corners of the ceremonial area, like nightclub bouncers.

MUSIC CUE: tambourine and trumpet drops out . . . the accordion plays solo, a playful, curious tune . . .

Flower Girls Evgenia (11) and Alina (7) enter, each with a huge white bag. They open the bags, then run joyously down the aisle steps as the bag releases HUNDREDS OF WHITE PETALS. They sit with their parents or legal guardians in the first row.

CELEBRANT: [Chris invites everyone to stand to greet the bride.]
Guests stand.

MUSIC CUE: The playful accordion music winds down . . . dramatic pause . . . then the Bride's jam begins. It's a long entrance walk down those steps at the Plaza, so the music starts small, then becomes a full-fledged wild jam with all musicians contributing—including Tom and Joan on maracas and the entire bridal party clapping—by the time she reaches the top of the aisle.

Bride Natalya enters, looking spectacular, escorted by her father, Dmitri, and her mother, Ekatarina. Mom and Dad bring Natalya just past the first row of seats, where they pause. Mom/Dad/Daughter have a moment (kiss/hug etc.).

Groom Ben steps forward, kisses her Mom. Ben shakes Dad's hand; Dad grips his hand too long, stares at him with a look of death, pulls him close, and whispers something into his ear. Dad lets Ben go. Ben looks shaken. Dad hands Natalya to Ben.

Ben escorts Natalya to the ceremonial matrimonial sweet spot where Chris is waiting while Mom and Dad take their seats.

MUSIC CUE: The music comes to a satisfying flourish as Chris speaks.

CELEBRANT: [Chris invites the guests to sit.]
Guests sit.
MOH arranges Natalya's dress if necessary.

Welcome

CELEBRANT: [Chris welcomes everyone, mostly in English, with one sentence in convincing Russian.]

Thanks

CELEBRANT: [Chris thanks everyone for coming.]

Parents

CELEBRANT: [Chris relays some loving sentiments from the couple to their parents.]

Honor Departed

CELEBRANT: [Chris briefly acknowledges departed family members who are deeply missed]

Love Story

CELEBRANT: [Chris tells a heartwarming, funny love story about Ben and Natalya, then introduces the vow section of the ceremony.]

Vows

BEN: Reads his vows to Natalya.

NATALYA: Reads her vows to Ben.

Rings

CELEBRANT: [Chris introduces the ring section of the ceremony.]
*Ring Bearer Samuel, age 8, enters, wearing a giant Bear head because he
is the* Ring Bear. *He hands Natalya's RING to Ben.*

CELEBRANT/BEN (repeating): I, Benjamin 'Fitzy' Fitzgerald, / take
thee, Natalya 'Velvet Cuffs' Trapeznikova, / to be my wedded wife, / to
have and to hold/ from this day forward, / for better, for worse, / for
richer, for poorer, / in sickness and in health, / to love and to cherish, /
till death do us part, / and if you die first, / I promise I will never love
another woman.
Ben slides the ring all the way onto her finger.
   *Ring Bear hands BEN'S RING to Celebrant, Celebrant hands it to
NATALYA.*
   Ring Bear hangs out nearby.

CELEBRANT/NATALYA (repeating): I, Natalya 'Velvet Cuffs' Trapeznikova, / take thee, Benjamin 'Fitzy' Fitzgerald, / to be my wedded
husband, / to have and to hold, / from this day forward, / for better, for
worse, / for richer, for poorer, / in sickness and in health, / to love and
to cherish, / till death do us part, / and if you die first, / that will be sad.
Natalya slides the ring all the way onto his finger.

Wedding Zen

CELEBRANT: [Chris talks Ben and Natalya through a brief meditation
so they remember every detail of this moment.]

Pronouncement/Kiss

CELEBRANT: [Chris pronounces Ben and Natalya married.]

Natalya and Ben kiss.

The guests go nuts!

Recessional

MUSIC CUE: Entire band riffs on 'Crazy Little Thing Called Love' by Queen.

Natalya and Ben eventually stop kissing but it . . . it takes a while.

Natalya retrieves her bouquet from the Maid of Honor. Natalya and Ben exit.

All members of the bridal party high-five guests as they exit.

Best Man and Maid of Honor exit.

Zach and Heather exit.

Antoine and Sandra exit.

Bill and Ellie exit.

Tom and Joan exit.

The two huge, muscular Nightclub-Bouncer Guys exit holding hands with the Flower Girls Evgenia and Alina.

Chris invites first row of honored guests to exit, bride's side first, groom's side second.

Chris exits.

Natalya and Ben live a long, happy life together.

◀ QUESTIONS FOR COUPLES ▶

Creating a wedding ceremony script requires teamwork between you—the two people getting married—and the lucky person performing your ceremony. It's a three-way tango. It's a *pas de trois*. A big part of the process involves you sharing information about your relationship with your celebrant. Every celebrant has their own unique questionnaire that they will ask you to fill out in order to learn what they need to learn about you. Questions are useful tools for illumination: they are lamps, candles, floodlights, spotlights, and stadium lights, shining upon treasures of information, stories, anecdotes, facts, ideas, and philosophies. I love questions. I'm the kind of person who will buy books full of questions. The best conversationalists ask good questions and the best questions really get people thinking. Deciding to get married and deciding whom to marry are some of the biggest decisions a person can make; these decisions deserve a whole lot of thinking.

Here, I've provided some questions that I use for my clients. Questions include matters of the heart as well as matters of logistics. Your answers to the questions provided will help your celebrant get to know you and to create your personal love story; they may also help you think of everything you need to think of.

Not all the information you give will find its way into the ceremony, but by the time your wedding day comes around, the person marrying you will know you so well that your guests will think he or she is an old friend; *in a way, he or she will be.* (One more reason that I LOVE my job: I make friends all the time.) Think about this: it is easier and more likely for your professional officiant to become a friend than it is for your friend to become a professional officiant.

Couples: use these questions to warm up for whatever questions *your* officiant will ask and to help you both think through the logistics of your ceremony.

Officiants: let these questions inspire your own questionnaire.

Remember, be forthcoming with your answers. Tell the truth. Provide as many details as you can. ("I love the way she makes banana pancakes" or "I love the way she takes the time to thank our waiter and say goodbye to them before we leave any restaurant" versus "I love the way she does stuff.") Try to avoid clichés. ("He makes every day worthwhile by making me feel valued" versus "He means the world to me.")

I. YOUR RELATIONSHIP:

How would you describe your fiancé(e) to me at a party if he/she was not at the party, and you were not allowed to take out your phone to show me pictures?

_____

_____

How long have you known each other/been together/been engaged?

_____

_____

How did you meet?

_____

_____

What do you remember about the very moment you met?

_____

_____

What do you remember about your first date, if you had a first date?

_____

_____

Using words, paint me a montage of highlights from the early days of your relationship.

_____

_____

Were there any obstacles to your relationship? What were they?

_____

_____

How are your personalities different from each other's?

_____

_____

How did you know you were in love? Was it fast? Was it gradual?

_____

_____

How did you propose or accept the proposal?

_____

_____

What do you love and admire about your fiancé(e)?

_____

_____

Looking back, what makes you proud of your relationship?

_____

_____

Are there any objects, colors, songs, symbols, articles of clothing, places, movies, genres, or expressions that symbolize and say something important about your relationship?

_____

_____

What is it like where you live? Are you in an apartment, a condo, a houseboat, a treehouse, an abandoned warehouse, some celebrity's garden, a yurt, a hotel . . . ?

_____

_____

II. THE WEDDING CEREMONY:

Date: _____ Time: _____

Location: _____ Approx. number of guests: _____

Will you have a rehearsal? If so, when? _____

Wedding party: First and last name, their relationship to you two; list all that apply

_____

_____

_____

_____

Escorts/Parents: Who, if anyone, will be escorting you into the ceremony? This is also a question for the groom! Parents usually enter near the beginning of the ceremony, either with or without the groom/bride, in various combinations.

_____

_____

Maid of Honor: _____

Matron of Honor: _____

Bridesmaids: _____

_____

Junior Bridesmaids _____

_____

Best Man: _____

Groomsmen: _____

_____

Flower Girl(s): _____ *Age(s)* _____

Ring-bearer(s): _____ *Age(s)* _____

What is your venue host's name and contact number?

_____

What is your photographer's name/company?

_____

What is your wedding planner's name and contact number (or day-of contact person)? _____

Why did you choose this particular venue?

_____

What has been the hardest thing about wedding planning?

_____

Will you be videotaping your ceremony? Who is the videologist?

_____

What music selections, if any, will you be having for the processional, bridal entrance and close of the ceremony (recession)?

_____

_____

Who are/is your musician(s) or DJ for the ceremony?

_____

Family Dynamics: What are your parents' names? Will they be at the ceremony? How long have they been married? If any of them are divorced or separated, fill me in.

_____

_____

What is your family heritage—ethnic, cultural, spiritual?

_____

_____

Are there any special customs or traditions from your heritage you would like to include in the wedding?

_____

_____

It's a pretty big deal to have your family and friends at your wedding ceremony, yes? Is there anything special that you would like them to know?

_____

_____

What are the various locations from which your guests will be traveling?

_____

_____

Would you like to include any words honoring your living parents or grandparents? If so, what would you like to be said?

_____

_____

Would you like to honor anyone who has passed away? If so, provide complete names and relationship to you.

_____

_____

Are there any readings you know you want to include? Would you like samples of readings? And if you do want to have a reading or two, do you have an idea of who your reader(s) will be?

_____

_____

Would you like to write personal vows to say to each other, would you like to say some formal/often-done vows, would you like me to do The

Asking (I ask several questions, you respond "I do"), or something else entirely?

_____

_____

What name do you want me to use in the ceremony—your first name or a nickname?

_____

_____

Will you be exchanging rings? Do they have a story?

_____

_____

Is there anything unusual that you'd like to try in your ceremony? I'm up for anything, and I'm always looking for new ways to make a ceremony dynamic. (For example, involving your Bridesmaids and/or Groomsmen, your musicians/DJ, video, pets, etc.)
What do you definitely not want for your ceremony?

_____

_____

III. YOU

Where did you grow up? _____
What was your high school/college/grad school/other?

_____

_____

What was your major in college/grad school?

_____

_____

What kind of jobs did you have, if any, during school?

_____

_____

What you do for a living now, and why do you do it?

_____

_____

Have you had any interesting career transitions in your life?

_____

_____

What is the motto or philosophy that you live by or would like to live by?

_____

_____

What are your honeymoon plans?

_____

_____

Are there any secrets we need to keep from the guests?

_____

_____

What would be the most surprising thing your guests could learn about you during the ceremony?

_____

_____

What things about you may I have fun with without embarrassing you?

_____

_____

WEDDING VOW WORKSHOP

Most of this book is meant to help you make a wedding ceremony unique, which will heighten the guest experience at a wedding, but uniqueness is not the most important thing. The most important thing is to remember to pay your vendors. (Kidding! Sort of.) At the heart of the entire enterprise of getting married is the game-changing connection that happens between two people.

When two people love each other constantly, when they find that their lives, their happiness, and their dreams are intertwined, and they decide that they would always like this to be the case, they should think about how to maintain this most powerful connection. Wedding vows outline the couple's plan for doing this.

The best weddings and the best wedding ceremonies are the best not for all the superficial showy trappings, not for the choices of decor, venue, food, drink, music, gifts, lighting, etc., but rather for the underlying truth that two people who love each other are getting married for all the right reasons.

As I've established, questions illuminate information; here, then, are some questions to consider when writing your vows:

Think of who you were as people back when you met versus who you are as people today: how have you changed? Do these changes make you feel proud? Do they surprise you? Do they affirm something you suspected from the very first moment you met?

What specific qualities of your partner do you most appreciate? Are these qualities things that you would also like to offer your partner?

What are the most grandiose, general things you would like your partner to have or experience?

What are the minutest, most specific things you would like your partner to have or experience?

Is there any kind of expression or thing to which you can allude that only the two of you would understand? Giving each other a private smile at this heightened moment in the ceremony is priceless.

Make a list of reactive actions, meaning, "When you do this, I will do that;" "When you are tired, I will make you coffee; when you are down, I will cheer you up; when your team loses the World Series in the bottom of the ninth inning of Game Seven on a walk-off grand slam by the other team's worst hitter, I will not console you with the phrase, 'There's always next season.'"

The Shape of Vows: A Thumbnail Sketch

Wedding vows are tough to write because they ought not to be too long. It's difficult for two people to consolidate and express all the emotions and goals that have for each other. A lot of people are not comfortable writing, expressing, or even accessing their emotions. Wedding vows require the heavy lifting of thinking, as does the very decision to get married. Couples often have no idea how vows should even sound, so here is a thumbnail sketch of how they go:

Start with a toe-in-the water introduction. This could be one or two short, sweet things you say about your partner. It could be a memory from the early days of the relationship or a significant moment. This short introduction can establish the theme of your vows, it can allow you to express something in simple language, and it can help you get your nervous mouth working before launching into the vows. This is not the time for promises, it's the time to say something beautiful. Doing this is much better than merely plunging into the vows.

Next: the actual vows. This can be a list, read as a list, one vow after another with no commentary. This can be a paragraph of phrasings as mentioned above (when you this, I will that) or explanations (because you always care for me, I will always take care of you). They can be a mixture of serious (I will comfort you when you are sick) and not-so-serious (I will always listen to you recap the phone call you just had even though I couldn't help overhearing the entire thing because you were right next to me and frankly you did most of the talking). As long as you are stating promises with or without commentary, these will count as vows.

Listing only one or two vows does not feel substantial—three is the bare minimum, but more is better, within reason. While I have no scientific number to aim for, keep an eye on how long your vows take, and let that guide you. Your vows could all be really short, in which case they will take less time to say and thus you may incorporate more of them; they may be long and overarching, in which case you will need fewer of them.

Finally, wrap up with one last sweet, loving statement, ideally using the word LOVE. Things like, "I am the luckiest person in the world. I love you, and I can't wait to call you my wife."

That's it. Keep it simple. Aim for sixty seconds. It will take you ninety seconds to two minutes, but aim for one minute. If you aim for two minutes, it will take three to four, and that's too long.

I cannot state strongly enough how important it is to WRITE your vows. The worst, sloppiest, least effective vows I've witnessed were ones where the person made them up on the spot or worked from a general outline in their head. Big mistake. Both times I've seen this, the vow-improviser cried a lot, was incomprehensible, and probably left out a lot of things he could have said. The idea of "speaking from the heart" may appeal to you, but please take my advice that this is far too important to not think through and write down ahead of time.

When you read your vows, read them from an actual notebook or piece of paper. Do not use your phone—the ol' tact-o-meter explodes when people try to read off their phone. There is a whole cottage industry for vow books. Get yourself something important and meaningful, and read the vows right off whatever you choose.

DO NOT TRY TO MEMORIZE THEM. This is not about showing off your memorization skills, and why risk forgetting to say something in the only time you really need to say it?

And here is my biggest tip for you: HAVE YOUR CELEBRANT HELP YOU. Whenever I help clients write their vows, I have them keep them a secret from each other, working with me on separate email chains. This way, each of them only hears the other's vows during the actual wedding. And this way, I can be the arbiter of length and tone, advising them whether they need to add words or cut words. This way, both of your vows will ROCK. Feel free to reach out to me for vow consultations!

WEDOPEDIA

An A to Z glossary of buzzwords that couples will encounter during the hazing ritual we call "planning a wedding."

♥

A I S L E : The aisle is the walkway between the two rectangles of seats, where the bridal party walks slower than they usually do into the ceremonial area.

The aisle is a function of practicality because otherwise, the bridal party would have to enter around the sides of the guests or be lowered from the ceiling. Those are literally the only options. It's also a way to separate the groom's family from the bride's family. This has long been the practice, just in case the two families are at war with each other. (Hmmm: instead of a border wall, maybe a border aisle?)

On the other hand, the aisle need not be the DMZ of wedding spaces. Lots of couples' families get along just fine, and guests are often invited to 'pick a seat, not a side, we love you all, thin or wide.' Close family members are usually separated each to a side, but this is purely a practical way to ensure that all parents have seats of honor in the front row.

No law states that there must be only one aisle in a wedding. Should anyone involved in your wedding want to get creative with chair set up, you could create diagonal entranceways, sideways entranceways, or any other setup that could subvert expectations. Instead of one focal aisle, you can create the excitement of wondering who will walk down which aisle. As long as there are enough chairs for all the expected guests, and each guest has a good view of the ceremony, set them up any old way you want. Incorporate platforms. Decorate the chairs with flowers or lights or balloons. Use chairs that don't match, chairs that aren't the same style.

A LTA R : The area at the front of the ceremonial space where the ceremony takes place. I prefer to call it the "ceremonial matrimonial sweet spot," which I think is catchier than "Love's Trap Door."

AM I OUT OF MY MIND?: (See OUTDOOR WEDDINGS)

A S K I N G , T H E : Some couples don't want to say personal vows out loud at their wedding. For some, this is just too personal for them, despite the fact that they made 150 friends and family members travel across the country and book hotel rooms and buy gifts and dress up in tuxedos and show up for a long night of catered food and canned dance music in order to help them celebrate something very personal.

For these people, a good solution is The Asking, in which the celebrant asks a series of questions that amount to vows. The couple responds, individually, with the words "I do." (See also Chapter 8 on page 86 and Sample Ceremony: Ben and Natalya on page 132.)

BACHELOR PARTY: The bachelor party originated in Sparta in the fifth century BC, on a Thursday. Or maybe it originated elsewhere. I don't know, I'm not a history professor. I do know that the bachelor party is the last chance a groom is allowed to misbehave without consequences. It is a celebration of HEdonism: Drugs, alcohol, strippers, bro-hugs, more strippers, bellicose professing of man-ness—these are all marks of a good bachelor party. If the groom and other participants have little recollection of what happened the next day, all the better. I believe there is a film (or several) inspired by the idea of a bachelor party gone wrong.

The best man has a lot on his shoulders when planning his friend's bachelor party because if it's boring, his entire maleness will be in question for the rest of his life. If the best man is floating the idea of a tea service followed by a knitting class at the local library, it's time to find another best man. If the best man and all the groomsmen show up at the groom's house on Harleys, with the Philly Phanatic leading the pack, the groom is in for an adventurous evening (especially if none of them know how to ride a motorcycle).

The bachelor party's subtext is the question: "Are you suuuuuuuuure you want to get married?" The answer to that question should be: "Yes, I am absolutely sure," which is why it is the best man's responsibility to make sure the groom feels completely horrible the next morning. The bachelor party is behavioral therapy, in that hedonism is paired with a crushing hangover. Hedonism is therefore associated with pain and henceforth avoided. (In theory.)

BACHELORETTE PARTY: Also called a "Hen" Party. (Hens call them "Bock Bock Bakawwwwww!") A hen party is a celebration of SHEdonism. At a bachelorette party, the bride's friends and sisters will go out, drink too much, shout "woo hoo!," do shots of Jägermeister, and dance on top of a bar, like in *Coyote Ugly*. The women will decorate themselves in a ridiculous corruption of traditional bridal gear. There will be drama. At least one of them will lose their smartphone. They will take selfies and dance in the exact same way to different kinds of dance music. (Hands in the air, moving their hips in a way they saw someone moving their hips in a video.) Each of them, throughout the evening, will confess to how beautiful the bride is, even when the bride is sitting on the floor of the ladies' room with a black eye and vomit trickling down her chin.

Men in public who encounter a bachelorette party in progress would be well advised to step away, the way one side-steps a spilled smoothie because maybe it's not a smoothie.

The subtext for every Bachelorette Party is "woooooo-hooooo!!!!!!"

BREAKING OF THE GLASS: Everyone loves yelling "Mazel Tov!" People incorporate the phrase "mazel tov" into daily conversation. Some people shorten it to "mazel." My friend Taj likes to say, "Mazel Taj." It's a fun, exotic way of saying good luck, or good for you, or thanks for the free dinner. Everyone loves yelling out loud if they know everyone else will be yelling out loud too. Everyone loves that they can be outgoing and anonymous at the same time. (Also why people move to New York.)

The breaking of the glass, from the Jewish faith, symbolizes the fragile nature of love. Love is very fragile and, once broken, is hard to put back together again. In other words, it's not a good idea to make your wife shatter into thirty-five pieces, so don't put her into a wood chipper. In other-other words, treat your relationship as if it has the tensegrity of an expensive wine glass or a small filament light bulb. Assume your marriage will shatter at the slightest provocation. The breaking of the glass casts a skeptical eye on most relationships as if they're just moments from disaster.

What would make more sense is if instead of breaking a glass, we make the couple *reassemble* a glass that is *already broken*, so they get a good taste of what a pain it would be to have to mend a shattered relationship. I mean *anyone* can shatter a glass and ruin a relationship. Just saying. I think they've got it backward.

♥

CERTIFIED LIFE-CYCLE CELEBRANT®: A trained, certified Life-Cycle Celebrant can make your wedding ceremony an extravaganza of personal storytelling, romance, and joy. Celebrants train at the prestigious and little-known Celebrant Foundation & Institute. Becoming a celebrant is a great career idea for people who have lived a bit, for middle-aged people or seniors transitioning from full-time work to part-time work, or retired people whose spouses have been pleading with them to get out of the house.

Celebrants learn the art of ceremony, storytelling, public speaking, rituals, interpersonal juggling, spiritual traditions, cultural idiosyncrasies and self-promotion. They also spend a lot of time learning to pronounce the word "celebrant" so people don't think they're talking about being "celibate," which is a totally different thing. (Do celibate people celebrate anything?)

Celebrants know what they're doing. They've encountered every type of couple (old and young, tall and short, right-wing and left-wing, smart and dumb, Aquarius and Capricorn), every type of ceremony situation (second marriage, third marriage, outdoor, indoor, big crowd, small crowd, mic, no mic), every combination of spiritual beliefs (Jewish and Catholic, Christian and Muslim, Atheist and Agnostic, Wicca and Mormon, etc.). When you are thinking about hiring someone to officiate your ceremony, ask yourself these questions:

> **Do I have one or more spiritual or cultural elements in my ceremony that require acknowledgment in a dignified manner?**
> Answer: Hire a trained Life-Cycle Celebrant™.
>
> **Do I want my ceremony to kick the evening off on a high-energy celebratory note?**
> Answer: Hire a trained Life-Cycle Celebrant™.
>
> **Do I want to spend top dollar to hire a professional to over-deliver on quality?**
> Answer: Hire a trained Life-Cycle Celebrant™.
>
> **If I hire a dentist to do my root canal, and I hire an accountant to do my taxes, and I hire a mechanic to fix my transmission, and I hire a lawyer to represent me in court, what kind of professional should I hire to create and perform my wedding ceremony?**
> Answer: Hire a trained Life-Cycle Celebrant™.

CHUPPAH: A chuppah is a rectangular, four-pillared open roof that stands in, and visually dominates, the ceremonial space. The open roof represents the home of the about-to-be-married couple, the hospitality that they had better pay their relatives if they know what's good for them, and the openness of spirit the couple must have with their family. In other words, the Chuppah reminds the couple to be prepared for drop-ins.

COCKTAIL HOUR: Have an open bar. (See also OPEN BAR)

DAY-OF COORDINATOR: Unless you would like to be stressed out of your mind on your wedding day, you should hire a day-of coordinator to handle all the functional details so you can concentrate on enjoying yourself and/or rethinking your decision to marry.

A day-of coordinator is a detail-obsessed organizer with managerial experience who loves to orchestrate the work of multiple vendors. She's usually a woman, no idea why. She'll be a lifesaver on your wedding day. She'll be the one to answer phone calls and texts while you have your photo taken with your fiancé(e) in a gritty alleyway in DUMBO or a meadow in Montana. She'll handle staff questions while you get drunk in the back of your limousine on the way to another part of your photo shoot. She'll make sure the band knows when to arrive and where to set up when they do. She'll make sure the florist finishes decorating the ceremonial area in time for your photographer to take pre-ceremony shots while you boogie with your besties to Beyoncé in your bridal suite. She'll make sure you and your fiancé(e) get to eat something before that social whirlwind you'll face at the reception. She'll do it all with a smile on her face, no matter how crazed the day seems because she lives for this adrenaline. She thrives on it. I don't know how she gets through the rest of her week, or why she is always a woman.

DESTINATION WEDDING: A wedding in a distant, inconvenient location to which nobody can afford to go.

DIAMONDS: Diamonds are forever, meaning, it'll take you forever to pay for a diamond. (See also KARAT) Diamonds are a good test to see how superficial your girlfriend really is. Any round object imbued with your love that fits around her finger should be enough for her to understand that you intend to love her forever, even if it's just an onion ring. If your girlfriend puts extraordinary pressure on you to produce a ring with a big diamond, let that be a preview of what her other expectations will be of you going forward.

If your girlfriend wants you to spend a fortune on a gaudy ring chock-full-o'-diamonds as a way of proving your love for her, my advice would be to reevaluate your wedding thoughts as soon as possible. (Buddy, if she can't love you for you…)

Spending a lot of money on a diamond is like a baseball team's general manager overspending on a closer. Sure, such an expenditure may pay dividends at important junctures in the immediate future, but in the long-term, don't be mistaken: no matter how great that ring is, you're going to have to come through in dozens of other ways.

As we establish in our sure-to-be-Pulitzer-Prize-winning section "Rings," there is great meaning and symbolism in rings. This part is just about the diamond. If you want to get your partner a diamond ring, for whatever reason, do it the right way. Go to a jeweler. Do your own research. Learn about the four C's: cut, clarity, cost, and Costco.

Cut: how many African children cut their hands finding this diamond?

Clarity: the degree to which your relationship is based on your diamond selection should offer you clarity as to whether this woman is for you.

Cost: what could you buy for the cost of this glittery piece of jewelry? Could you put someone through college? Could you feed a family in Africa? Could you buy season tickets to see your favorite sports team? What will other things cost during your marriage? You know, important things like houses and your daughter's wedding.

Costco: does Costco have a diamond department? Would your fiancée really know the difference if you bought a fake?*

*Yes, she would.

♥

E L O P E M E N T : I don't get why more people don't elope. People who elope are the smartest people in the world when it comes to wedding intelligence. We in the wedding industry don't want our industry disappearing, but we have to tip our hats to the geniuses who figure out that you can get married without the hoopla and expense. All you need are a few signatures on a license, a little bit of cash, some valid ID, and you can get married just as much as the couple that books the Park Plaza, hires the most heralded caterer, the hippest DJ, the best photographer, the most expensive videographer, and me.

Couples have all kinds of reasons to elope. Some of them love the romance of a distant, private wedding. Others can't afford a big to-do like the freaking Rockefellers. Some of them do not get along with their family. These are all valid reasons for eloping (and the last one is a good reason for therapy). Saying that you eloped is like saying you bought a Mercedes for $100. Eloping also saves your friends tons of money on travel and gifts. Everybody wins with elopements . . . *except* your family members who have waited their entire lives for the chance to meddle in your wedding plans and will now go to their grave knowing you no longer love them. Other than them, everybody wins with elopements... except most people in the wedding industry other than officiants, who can make half their money in one-tenth the time. I don't know algebra, but I suspect that's good math.

Couples can elope, then still organize and go through with a gigantic wedding. Why wait to reap the tax benefits of being a married couple? A lot of couples spend a year or more planning their big wedding—it may be that the tax benefits they'd get by being married during that year and a half could offset some of the expense of the wedding. In fact, I may start using that as an incentive for people to hire me twice.

♥

FIFTY PLACES TO WED YOUR LOVER:

A place of which you're fond
A gazebo by a pond
A lounge at a hotel
To the tune of Pachelbel
At a county jamboree
On a tour of NBC
A sunny leafy vineyard
A rustic goofy junkyard
At the place where you first met
In the rain so you get wet
A theater on a stage
A home where people age
A park before dark
An ark with Marky Mark
On the edge of a cliff
In between graveyard shifts
A barn on a horse
In Norway, where they're Norse
Your favorite casino
A gondola with Gino
The seventeenth green
A big trampoline
A catering hall
A new shopping mall
A rustic Brooklyn winery
An equation if you're binary

Against your parents' wishes
An aquarium of fishes
A cruise ship near Gibraltar
A cheesy makeshift altar
A pond, in the nude
A place where beer is brewed
A big skating rink
A concert with Pink
A café on the river
An igloo while you shiver
The Parthenon in Greece
Alaska, wearing fleece
Your building's cafeteria
Surrounded by wisteria
A church with a priest
Wearing khakis that are creased
A car by Lamar
A bar by a Czar
Times Square on New Year's Eve
A fundraiser with Steve
The place they cut your hair
A campsite with a bear
A lobster shack in Maine
A speeding Amtrak train

FIRST LOOK: "First Look" is easier to say than "first time the couple sees each other wearing the clothing they will wear at the wedding." Some people think that it's bad luck for the groom to see the bride in her wedding dress before the ceremony. (Definitely bad luck to see the groom in the wedding dress.) Some people think that if you step on a crack, you'll break your mother's back, despite a complete lack of cause and effect evidence. Some people believe that bad things will happen if you walk under a ladder. Are you the type who does not believe that, or who does? (Are you the former, or . . . the ladder?) It's also very difficult to prove that the groom seeing the bride in her bridal dress before the ceremony will lead to bad luck. It can be surmised that any bride or groom who believes in such a thing may in fact court bad luck for other cockamamie beliefs, so in that way, there's some validity to it.

Chris, what is the first look, exactly?
I should probably explain what this is, huh? Good point! Thanks goodness you're paying attention.

The First Look is for couples who see no credence in the groom-not-seeing-the-bride-in-her-wedding-dress-before-the-wedding superstition, and who care about guest experience. The First Look *is*, in fact, the first time a couple sees each other in their wedding attire, but the major difference is that this happens during a pre-ceremony photo shoot. The First Look is staged early, captured on camera, and then everyone can behave normally. After the ceremony, the couple can mingle with their guests whenever they're ready, and nobody has to go nuts hiding humans from each other. When couples eschew the solution of a First Look and instead need to be hidden from each other before the ceremony, it creates two challenges:

Challenge #1: The staff at the wedding venue, on top of everything else they have to arrange and stay on top of in order to produce the perfect wedding day they've promised, have to hide one human being from another, meaning they have to manage sightlines, corners and rooms, and maintain walkie-talkie contact with staff members assigned to each party.

Challenge #2: A lot of photographs will have to be taken after the ceremony, which means that the bridal party misses cocktail hour entirely, and all the guests who have traveled halfway around the world to attend your wedding now have to wait an additional hour to ninety minutes to see the only two people they really care about seeing that day.

What was that groaning sound?
Oh that was just Grandma—Grandmas get *really squeamish* about the groom not seeing the bride in her bridal outfit before the wedding.

Maybe Grandma needs to lighten up.
YOU tell her that.

F R I E N D : Some folks out in the world want to be married by a friend, someone who already knows them, someone they trust, and whom they don't have to pay much if anything. Friends can make a wedding ceremony feel like a casual, low-stress event.

If you have been asked to officiate your friend's wedding, congratulations! I hope this book helps you do justice to this undertaking. They may have asked you to officiate because you're the most outgoing person they know, or because you're a comedian, or because you introduced them to each other. No matter how extroverted you may be, there is, as I hope this book shows, a lot to consider when preparing and performing a wedding. Please do not hesitate to contact me through my website, www.IlluminatingCeremonies.com, if you would like to schedule a phone call tutorial. Operators are standing by (probably, somewhere. I don't employ any. Maybe I will be standing by). Please have your Venmo or Paypal account handy. Perhaps this will become my next big side business! Get in on the ground floor.

♥

GARTER: A piece of fabric meant to hold up stockings or socks. In the wedding sense, the garter is an item of clothing that the bride wears around her thigh. During the reception, the groom traditionally removes his bride's garter, then tosses it towards his unmarried male guests. Whoever catches it, according to tradition, will be the next to become married. Removing the garter symbolizes deflowering, not that anybody talks about that at the wedding. But now you have an icebreaker to use. You're welcome.

GUEST EXPERIENCE: Guest experience is a thing that begins long before your wedding day. Guest experience begins the moment the guests find out that they are guests. Here is a dramatization of that moment:

Average person stands in a ho-hum hallway, going through his mail.

"Here I am, merely a human being, opening some mail."

Opens your wedding invitation, reads it.

"Wait! I'm not just a human being! I'M A GUEST!"

Jumps in the air to click his heels, it's so awkward that he falls over, knocks over furniture

"I'm okay! I'm a guest now."

Guest experience is the kind of thing that can make it seem like the easiest, most fun thing in the world to buy every single thing requested on your wedding registry, including the extra-large wok, the set of Martha Stewart flatware and an apron that says, "Caution: Man Cooking."

Guest experience invites a domino-effect of karma and philanthropy (Karmanthropy). Guests could remember how they felt at your wedding and that good feeling could encourage benevolence, empathy, and volunteerism. I'm saying that a positive guest experience at a wedding could help make the world a better place. I'm saying that good guest experience could save the world. (Well, it sure wouldn't hurt.)

What improves guest experience/saves the world? Quality drinks. Plentiful food. Short lines at food stations and bars. Heavily passed drinks and snacks. Live musicians. Humor. Pleasant surprises. Gifts. Swag. Attention to detail. A funny celebrant who knows what he or she is doing. A venue that is the kind of place to which guests never go. A venue where the guests can walk from the ceremony to the cocktail hour in less than 60 seconds. Personalized place settings. Welcomes specific to geography, nationality, and language. A mix of the familiar and unfamiliar. Excuses to let hair down. A venue with views and photo ops. An Instagram station, including a frame with all the pertinent details of hashtaggery. An expertly designed cake and an impressive gluten-free, sugar-free cake for your dieting and diabetic friends.

And thanks—always expedite thanks. Spread thanks through the room with frequency, authenticity, and specificity.

♥

HANDFASTING: Go back far enough in history, and this is how people referred to weddings. This also refers to the symbolic act of binding the couple's hands together during a ceremony. There is nothing fast about a Handfasting. (See also KNOT, TYING THE)

HASHTAGS: Hashtags are a fun way to group all the photos your guests take at your wedding on Instagram so everyone can see how much fun everyone else was having and so you can have a free photo album that makes you wonder why you hired a photographer. #SpendMoreOnYourCelebrant

They are also an excellent opportunity to practice summarizing your wedding theme in one clever phrase. As Mark Twain wrote, "I didn't have time to write a short note, so I wrote a long one." Even Mark Twain had a hard time with hashtags. Brevity is hard to accomplish. This is why people who work in advertising make the big bucks. The good news is, if ever there was a time to think up puns, this is it!

#JoeAndKellyGetMarried (pretty on-the-nose)
#JoePutARingOnIt (better—Beyoncé reference)
#LivingInSinclair (now we're having pun)
#SingleNoMore (nice reference to Gallow Green's *Sleep No More*, which is itself a take on *Macbeth*)
#LoveAtDurstSite (play on words if you marry Fred Durst)
#JaneysGotAGunderson (whipping out the Aerosmith reference)
#TheWrightStuff (this feels so Wright)
#MyOldManning (nice play on "old man" and the last name of a former football quarterback)

#DoveActually (referencing a famous love movie by changing "love" to the groom's last name in exactly one letter)

The Wedding Hashers (www.weddinghashers.com) is a PHENOMENAL site to visit if you are stumped with your own hashtag. They employ professional writers to come up with hashtags in bunches for you. I am one of their writers. #ShamelessPlug #FortBrag #HasherIBarelyKnowEr

(See also INSTAGRAM)

♥

I M A M : A Muslim cleric, someone who stands in front of everyone in a mosque and leads prayers. Islamic wedding practices vary around the world.

I N Q U I R Y : Every vendor/client relationship begins with an inquiry. On The Knot, the boilerplate goes like this: "Hi! I found you on The Knot and would love more information on your services and pricing."

This site-generated text is completely impersonal. This sends a message to the vendor that you are incapable of writing a sentence on your own, have no idea how the world really works, and that you are probably just trying to reach out to lots of vendors with as little effort as possible. While your vendor may overlook this, chances are you have already turned off a professional who might have been a really good fit for your wedding.

To help forge a connection with a vendor who looks like they may be a great match for your wedding, reach out with a personal inquiry, one that shows that you have researched this vendor, and that you have a specific reason for reaching out to them.

Try this approach: "Hi [specific vendor's name], I found your listing on The Knot, read some of your reviews, went to your website, loved what I saw, and feel as if your unique, personal style is just what my fiancé(e) and I are looking for in a wedding vendor. We would love to speak with you on the phone at your earliest convenience."

I N S T A G R A M : Instagram is a social sharing site for photos and videos. Using your smartphone, you can, for example, take a photo of the ceremonial space, post it on your Instagram page, and wait for the adulation from your followers to roll in. Instagram etiquette suggests you give credit to all vendors involved in the wedding, whether via directly listing their Instagram name or by including them in a hashtag. A hashtag (#, the thing that looks like a tic-tac-toe board—if you are under age thirty-five, you are probably insulted that I am describing what a hashtag is. I sincerely apologize if I have offended you) is a grouping mechanism that allows you to focus your search within Instagram so you can see all the photos associated with a particular wedding. (Older people: think of it as the name of a folder, only you're not allowed to use spaces between words.)

On Instagram, other users can 'heart' your post, comment on your post, share your post, or ignore your post. Each heart and comment fuels your sense of self-worth. Each poorly received post deflates your ego and makes you feel like you're at a party with nobody to talk to. (Instaglum.)

(See also HASHTAGS)

INVITATION: Invitations are the things sent out to guests to let them know you'd like them to be present at your wedding. Invitations are perhaps the hardest thing to figure out other than deciding who to marry. Who will you invite to your wedding? Who will you NOT invite? These are sensitive questions and must be agonized over with mothers. If you have no mothers available, find girlfriends. Every angle of invite or non-invite must be examined so thoroughly that one or both of you will become an alcoholic before the wedding day. (If you are already an alcoholic: get help.)

An invitation to attend a wedding is a flattering outreach of love. If you agree to attend, you agree that you will make babysitting, flight, hotel, rental car, and other arrangements and not give the couple a hard time about any of it because you would expect them to do the same for your wedding.

♥

JUDGE: A person wearing a giant black robe who performs wedding ceremonies at the City Clerk's office. Judges' weddings are some of the fastest, least expensive, most perfunctory, and least personal in the land. People who get married by a judge tend to be either in a hurry (perhaps a military deployment is imminent), financially unable to have a large wedding, hiding from their families, or all the above. Not that there's anything wrong with any of these scenarios. (And thank you to our military for serving our country.)

JUMPING THE BROOM: Jumping the broom is a curious wedding tradition popular among African Americans because . . . well, it is difficult to determine why. Research proves conflicting. Some say the tradition comes from Ghana. Some say it comes from Scotland, others say it comes from Wales. Some say slave owners used to make slaves jump over a broom in their wedding ceremony just to mock them. Some say the broom represents the couple bonding with the domestic life, which of course included brooms. Some say the broom represents sweeping away the past to clear a way for a new life. Some say it reminds them of a time when slaves were not allowed to legally marry. Some say the splayed-out part of the broom represents all the other people at the wedding, and the long handle represents the couple, which does not explain the jumping. Some say brooms were waved above the couple's head to ward off spirits, which also does not explain the jumping part. Some say it represented the bride's agreement to sweep out the courtyard. I don't know too many brides who would be nuts about that idea.

Still others see jumping over the broom as a way to defy witchcraft.

It may be that this tradition will mean something else entirely in a hundred years; rituals can morph and change along with the people who practice them.

Generally, the notion of sweeping away the old to welcome what's new is pretty clean symbolism. Crossing a threshold is certainly what couples do when they become married, so jumping over a broom is a tidy symbolism twofer.

I think it would be pretty unique to watch a couple jump over a broom, especially the bride, if she forgets to remove her delicate high heels before she jumps. And I think it would be downright culturally apt for a half-African (or half-Welsh) half-Jewish couple to combine rituals by jumping over a broom . . . and landing on a glass, thus breaking it.

 To me the jumping part is the most entertaining, so why not accentuate the jump with a trampoline? And the landing should really spark something visually and auditory stimulating like a light show and music; let the landing kick-off a celebration.

And why stop at a broom? Why not an entire obstacle course? Once marriage begins, the jumping just keeps on going, and some hurdles are more difficult than others. Boxes of diapers, piles of tax forms, calendars, keys, real estate brokers, stethoscopes, so many things can symbolize life thresholds and most of these things can be jumped over. (Underscore every jump with opening synth chords of Van Halen's "Jump.")

♥

KARAT: A karat is a unit of measurement for diamonds. The higher the number of karats, the more superficial the bride is and/or the less confident the groom is in the bride and/or the more the groom hopes the bride will forgive him his future frugality.

Karat cake is not a thing, but it would be a great title for the wedding cake. Just put a big sign by it that says "Karat Cake." It's about diamonds, but it's gold.

(See also DIAMONDS)

K A R M A : Karma is the surveillance video of your entire life. Karma sees everything. Yes, even that. It is an invisible world force that feeds on and affects itself in equal and opposite balance based on what one puts out into the world. If a person puts good vibes out into the world, good vibes will come back to that person in equal measure.

For example, if a person performs an act of selfless, generous kindness for a stranger, it may be that the love of their life might walk right around the corner, sweep that selfless person off their feet and marry them. On the other hand, if a person does something mean to a co-worker, like replace his real coffee with decaf, the love of their life might walk right around the corner, sweep them off their feet, marry them and then, months later, reveal that he or she is, in fact, the worst tipper they've ever seen. Like, embarrassingly cheap.

K N O T , T H E : The Knot is the place where all wedding vendors should advertise. Their hefty print publication could be used as a doorstop or to clobber someone who doesn't tip well. Their online presence is at www.theknot .com. I owe most of my career to The Knot. I love The Knot. I am Knot-ical. I am Knotty by nature. I am tied to The Knot. I do not have a sponsorship deal with The Knot (yet!).

You could spend days on The Knot website searching for florists, photographers, caterers, DJs, musicians, portrait artists, counselors, venues, and officiants. In addition to providing a link to the absolute best in the business, they have a review-based system for allowing the cream of the crop to rise to the top of the mountain and shine like a star while angels sing and trumpets blare. Vendors who receive a certain number of positive reviews within a certain time frame win the coveted The Knot Best of Weddings award. Vendors who receive enough 'Best of' awards are voted into The Knot Hall of Fame.

The Knot is so important in the wedding industry (HOW . . . IMPORT-ANT . . . IS IT?) I made a list of explanatory comparisons. Find the one that appeals to you!

- For my baseball fan audience: The Knot is the Yankees of weddings.
- For my football fan audience: The Knot is the New England Patriots of weddings.

- For my basketball fan audience: The Knot is the Michael Jordan of weddings.
- For my hockey fan audience: The Knot is the Wayne Gretzky of weddings.
- For my European Soccer fan audience: The Knot is the Real Madrid of weddings.
- For my financial page audience: The Knot is the Warren Buffett of weddings.
- For my comedy-loving audience: The Knot is the Stephen Colbert of weddings.
- For my jewelry-loving audience: The Knot is the Tiffany's of weddings.
- For my five-star restaurant-loving audience: The Knot is the Noma of weddings.
- For my opera-loving audience: The Knot is the Luciano Pavarotti of weddings, only alive.
- For my theater-loving audience: The Knot is the Bette Midler in *Hello Dolly* of weddings.
- Actually, The Knot is if *Rent, The Producers, The Book of Mormon,* and *Hamilton* were all rolled into one show called *Hamilton Rents a Mormon Book Producer (Named Evan Hansen)*. It would be timely, socially conscious, historical, hilarious, have a dubious plotline, and would probably star Nathan Lane.
- For my French audience: The Knot is the France of weddings.

KNOT, TYING THE: The Knot is also something couples tie, literally, for symbolic reasons, during the handfasting ceremony. I get the symbolism. I don't need the symbolism, but I get the symbolism. The officiant, or a family member, or multiple family members, wrap a cord or rope or scarf or Christmas lights or duct tape or hockey skates around the couple's joined hands while saying poetic, meaningful things about them and marriage, and then finishes by tying a knot, symbolizing that the couple is bonded together. As they stand there with their hands tied, do they look like prisoners or kidnapping victims? Maybe. Would that suggest that marriage can be a prison or something into which people enter against their will? I don't know—why would anyone bring up such a thought? Jeez. At that point, someone should announce that the symbolism of the ritual is over because the next thing that happens is this: the couple extricates themselves from the knot, preserving the knot itself as a keepsake, a process designed to be easy—and, while this double-Houdini escape trick is not meant to be symbolic, it kinda can't help being so.

"Wow. They sure got out of those ropes easily. Was that part of it? Are we to believe that their bond is tenuous at best?"

"Please stop talking."

LIVE MUSIC: Even though there is a certain amount of security in having a DJ and recorded music, an assurance that the bands will hit all the right notes because you know they did while they were recording the music, having a live musician is a surefire way to make your wedding ceremony unique.

Live music played before the ceremony, as guests arrive, helps establish a mood. Classical music is classy, jazz is iconic, pop music is cheerful. String trios are great. Solo guitarists are great. Drummers are great. If I could, I'd have a street-drummer from a New York subway play before every wedding I officiate.

Plus, live musicians can elongate a song for a processional that takes longer than we think it will, or play surprise interludes during awesome love stories, or switch from pop to classical in a second. Live musicians lend an air of dignity to weddings that a huge black table covered in computers and wires can't.

LOVE: Love is a complicated thing. Love is a motivator, a jester, a raison d'être. Love underwrites weddings, at least, these days. In the past (and, still, sadly, today) many marriages were/are arranged, mere business transactions between families. Love is more of an active participant these days, at least in the free world.

Love makes people do things they would never do, say things they'd never say, buy things they'd never buy. Love inspires poets, cinematographers, and romance novelists. Love seduces the young, the old, and the people who are sort of getting old but tell people they are a few years younger than they really are. Love dissolves reason. Love finds solutions. Love heals. Love flows. Love must be like fish: moving forward with constant energy. Love goes well with music, sofas, and sunsets. Love happens when two grown adults are sitting in bathtubs that happen to be side by side in a field. Love reduces things to their essential soul. Love emerges like a butterfly's wings. Love adds spice like hot sauce to Buffalo wings.

Love reveals itself slowly. Love tackles you. Love was in front of you all along. Love calls long-distance. Love was calling from inside the house! Love is inside you. Love is in a pair of hands. Love is in a glance. Love is in every inch of Paris. (Paris, France that is. Paris, Texas is full of railroads.)

Love makes a person dedicate himself or herself to the eternal task of ensuring happiness for another human being, which then, in the best of circumstances, ensures happiness for the person who does the ensuring. (Life *Ensurance*) Love is a product of karma, and karma is a product of love.

I'd like to point out that I got through this whole section without mentioning that love is a battlefield. (So close!)

♥

MARRIAGE: Marriage is more than a booty call without the commute. It is completely outside the scope of this book. When people ask me to officiate their marriage, I point out that that would be impossible, because when it comes to syntax, I'm a jerk.

Planning a wedding is a hazing ritual that can give you a sneak-peek at marriage. You learn what you're each like when taking on a project. One of you may lead. You may divide tasks equally. One of you may do everything. One of you may be a little bit *too* into shopping for the dress, and it may not be the woman.

I'm glad people take a long time to plan their weddings because, in that time, they learn a lot about each other and encounter problems early on. When I hear about a wedding being canceled, I'm disappointed at first, but I'm happy that people identify their relationship weaknesses before they take the actual leap of getting married. This is also why my retainer fee is non-refundable.

MARRIAGE LICENSE: The marriage license is the most important object of the entire wedding. Sure, you might have spent $500 a piece on your table decorations, but the license, which costs all of $35 at the City Clerk's office (2018 New York prices; your City Clerk experience may differ), is the only thing that will help you transition from not married to totally married.

Of course, in a way, it costs more than $35; *it costs your entire life.* No pressure! Choose wisely. (#IDoDiligence)

Every state has a different way of handling marriage licenses. I advise couples to research what they need to obtain a marriage license first and foremost. It would be a shame to go through the whole wedding hazing ritual and come out of it not married because you never remembered to get your license. That's just stupid, although sure enough, I've seen it happen.

Signing the marriage license can be fun too. Always grab your photographers to get them to capture the signing. It is a Norman Rockwell-worthy moment, a tradition and rite of passage that all couples must go through. Jokes abound. Someone always says something like, "Don't do it!" or "You can still say no!" Sometimes that person is me. Sometimes I'm not joking. The jokes are nearly part of the license-signing ritual. And yet, the license is no joke. Signing the license is the only thing that has to happen for couples to be married. The rest is to make sure that everyone knows how important it is. (And to keep me and my colleagues employed.)

In Europe, it is common to sign the license during the ceremony; not so much in the states. Americans feel it's a bit of a time drag, mostly because it's a time drag. There is so much pressure to get to cocktail hour, and signing the license does take a few minutes that could be spent downing signature drinks. However, since New York attracts wedding couples from around the world, I do, on occasion, end up putting the signing into the ceremony. There are ways to make this fun: I invite absolute silence while each signer signs, like at a golf match as a golfer putts, then pandemonium upon each signing, signature by signature, until I sign at the end. I take inspiration from (meaning: I rip-off) Jimmy Fallon's "Thank You Notes" segment on *The Tonight Show,* with license-signing music and unnecessarily dramatic pauses, pen held aloft, then swiftly applied to paper.

Thank you, Jimmy Fallon, for giving me such an easy gag to rip off.

Sincerely, Every Wedding Officiant.

MARRY (VERB): to agree to share your life inside and out with another human being for the rest of your life and/or theirs. Forever. For eternity. You and your beloved. The two of you. That's it. Choose wisely. Good luck!

#AreYouSure, #MeasureTwiceCutOnce, #SocialConstruct

MATRIMONY: This is the state of being married. It is an *altar*ed state. (Send all your comments on this joke to me on the back of a ten-dollar bill.)

MEMORY BOXES: A memory box is a time capsule of love. Couples incorporate a memory box into their ceremony to ensure future sentiment and for emotional insurance in case of hard times. The memory box is literally a box, usually hand-crafted by an old man somewhere in Santa Fe or the Berkshires, designed to look attractive when displayed on mantelpieces, side tables, or toilets. Couples fill the memory box with all sorts of things, usually including a bottle of wine and a few letters. The wine might be a vintage from the vineyard where they got engaged, or from the wine store in Covington where they first dabbled in shoplifting. The letter might be something romantic or something to remind them of how happy they were on their wedding day or to remind them of what bad writers they were on their wedding day.

Some couples want language in the ceremony explaining that they intend to open the box on their fifth, tenth, fifteenth, or twentieth (etc.) anniversary.

Other couples are more skeptical (they open it after two weeks), and want language explaining that they intend to open the box, read the letters and drink the wine when their marriage is in trouble, or they've had a big fight, or one of them gets imprisoned for shoplifting. I'm not a fan of this approach—I understand that the letters within, read years after the trials of marriage have worn nerves thin, may revive the love that began it all, especially if they also down the whole bottle of wine on an empty stomach. I still don't like introducing any suggestion of negativity to the ceremony. That's just me. Just call me Positive Pauly. (No, don't. Don't ever call me that.)

We could make this unique! Guests can enter a betting pool, wagering on dates the couple will open the box. I mean if you're going to entertain negative thoughts, make the negative thoughts entertaining! Have the box locked and have the lock linked to an app that alerts all the guests the moment it's opened, with automatic links hooked up to the betting pool. There must be some scientific way to do this. Trademark! #WeddingMarchMadness

Other things I would *not* suggest putting into a memory box: a loaded pistol, a knife, a live bird, a photo of each other naked, a photo of your hot sister naked, any yogurt, your smartphone, your own prediction for your marriage fail date . . .

(See also RITUALS)

M O N E Y : This is a big one. This is one of the two biggest reasons anybody does anything, the other being sex. And when you combine sex and money, you've got something impossible to explain to your first or second wife. Money is a huge consideration for couples planning a wedding, and stating this is one of the biggest understatements of the year, not that there is an official competition for understatements. Although there should be. On average, couples spend between $17,000 and $77,000 on their wedding. I know, right? (I'm so glad for it! Keep spending, couples!!! Cha-ching!!!) Think of how many vacations you could go on for either of those amounts. Planning a wedding is a constant battle between what you want and what you or your parents can afford. Everything costs money. For some reason, even the most frugal couples toss their frugality out the window, where it splatters on the neighbor's window across the alley. People who regret spending $1 on Hostess cupcakes spend $1,000 on a cake. Couples who eat canned tuna for their only source of protein spend $8,000 on catering for their hundred guests. First of all, who invites 100 people to dinner and then picks up the bill? When it's wedding time, couples feel pressure to produce a huge event. Wedding professionals will do nothing to dissuade them from doing this.

Come to think of it, I'm a wedding professional.

Hey, you know what? You know all that money you have in the bank or invested in stocks? You should cash it all out and spend it on your wedding, or your child's wedding. Yeah. I read somewhere—maybe *Golf Digest*, maybe it was *Forbes Magazine*—that the more you spend on your wedding, the longer the glaciers will last.

MOTHER NATURE: Mother Nature is the angriest single mother. She is the original Diva. She is a fickle shrew determined to be the center of attention. Mother Nature loves outdoor weddings because that's when she gets to even the score. What score? Who knows? Like I said, she's fickle. Thanks to global warming, she's experiencing a prolonged menopause, so anything can happen. It could be too hot, it could be too cold, it could rain . . . it will do whatever the heck Mother Nature wants it to do. The earth is her show. You try to change her climate, she's going to change yours.

When people tell you that rain at a wedding is good luck, it's because they can't hear the music over your crying. When it's too hot and humid at a wedding, nobody tells you that it's good luck because they're too annoyed at you for holding an outdoor wedding during the summer with no air-conditioned indoor plan B.

❤

NON-ALCOHOLIC BEVERAGES:

Similes:

Sugar-free chocolate

Weapon-free military

Jim Belushi

On the one hand: why?

On the other hand, non-alcoholic beverages are useful for children, and recovering alcoholics. People on restrictive diets might like them; try to seat those people together.

NUPTIALS: A word used to refer to a wedding when you are really sick of using the word "wedding" or are trying to sound chummy with a buddy at the trucker bar without revealing that you secretly crave a wedding as elaborate as Princess Diana's even though on a macro level that whole thing did not end well.

"Me 'n Margie's doin' our nuptials in August down on the dock."

"August? Gonna be hot as my armpits in the attic while I'm hidin' from my mother-in-law. You got an air-conditioned indoor plan B?"

"Nope."

"Then I can't make it, sorry."

"I ain't even tol' you the date yet."

"Look at the time. Gotta walk ma' dawg." [drops a ten on the counter, leaves]

"You don't have a dawg..."

♥

OBJECTIONS: I have no problem with objections. I object to questions about objections in a ceremony. You know the scenario: late in the ceremony, the person presiding over the wedding asks if anyone sees any reason why this man or woman should not be married to this woman or man. Everyone glances around the room, and then the movie's hero stands up, tells the bride he's always loved her, that he can't see her marry this putz, a huge fight ensues, and when the melee ends, the hero is in the bride's arms in the back of a school bus, while guests continue to set things on fire behind them.

In olden days, this question may have been a good one, one last shot for reason to prevail. But really, why would anyone *wait until the wedding* to object? The time to object was during the engagement period after your eighteen-year-old daughter decided to marry her fifty-year-old Biology teacher.

A clever officiant could fake people out, and then ask, "Does anyone object to ... HAVING FUN?" Then start the cocktail hour with a Bon Jovi anthem and a balloon drop.

OFFICIANT: An officiant is someone who has become licensed in a particular state or states to legally solemnize weddings. They are likely to have a performance background, or some cursory training in some kind of spiritual practice. They are men, except when they are women.

A divorced officiant would be an example of irony. (Not to Alanis Morissette.) (Hi kids! That's what we call a '90s reference!)

OLD MAN: A way a wife may refer to her husband.

OLD LADY: A way a husband may refer to his wife if he enjoys being pummeled with a skillet.

OUTDOOR WEDDINGS: Outdoor weddings sound romantic. A sun-swept lawn, a ceremony space framed by trees, a lazy river rolling along behind it all. It seems like a photogenic, picture-perfect idea. How lovely it will be to hear a light breeze whispering through the trees, the gentle buzz of cicadas, and the warmth of the sun on your face as you join together in matrimony with the love of your life.

This idyllic fantasy does happen in real life, it really does. In general, though, if you decide to have an outdoor wedding, and you have no indoor or sheltered Plan B, you are risking a lot.

Imagine an outdoor ceremony space in the month of August, or even July, or June, or September. The grass is uneven, making walking in high heels or after the age of seventy difficult. The sun is out, not a cloud in the sky, and not due to set for another two or three hours. The heat is piercing and relentless. The humidity rests on everyone like a layer of expired butter. A few hundred mosquitoes are having their own wedding party at the same venue. Everyone is wearing fancy clothing—fancy, heavy, hot clothing. Shirts are sticking to backs, armpits are soaked, and I don't even want to suggest what's happening *down there.*

Your guests feel disgusting. Some of them have not eaten in hours, in hopes that they will fit into the sexiest clothing they own. They are dehydrated. They are squinting directly into the sun. Bugs are buzzing by their heads. Young Jeremy got stung by a bee. Aunt Emma swatted at a mosquito, missed, and instead sliced Uncle Jim's cornea. None of them are paying attention to the ceremony. Instead, they are focusing their ire on you for choosing to hold an outdoor ceremony. In their minds, they are composing emails they may never send to you. They are swearing under their breath. They are swearing over their breath. They are taking the Lord's name in vain and embellishing his name with inappropriate middle names. Grandmas are rethinking their wills. The wine in the memory box is going sour. The unity candle is more symbolic of the guests' shared annoyance at you than your unity. The officiant is thinking about how he should have charged you more, even if only to cover his dry-cleaning.

Imagine if you'd forked over $150 to see a hit Broadway play, but they'd decided to hold it in an outdoor venue in the middle of August. Wouldn't you want your money back? Why risk the biggest production of your life to the whims of Mother Nature? Everyone knows that Mother Nature is exhausted, temperamental, and smokes five packs a day.

I can't think of any other situation in which people would invite people to sit for thirty minutes or longer (lots of people arrive early) in a baking hot space *and* have the balls to tell them the event is black tie. Why would anyone make their grandmother sit inside a sweat lodge? Who in their right mind would make their poor groomsmen stand in the blinding sunlight for a whole ceremony? Somehow, the fact that it's a wedding is supposed to make it okay? It is not okay. It is cruel.

People say, "Oh, but I've always dreamed of having an outdoor wedding." I get it—I've dreamed of things too, but dreams are often not realistic. Just because you've dreamt of something doesn't mean it can or should happen.

Here are some outdoor wedding realities:

- Outdoor wedding on a beach: a strong wind flopping dresses, veils and ceremony pages every which way, whipping sand into people's faces, sunlight piercing the epidermal layer of everyone present.
- Outdoor wedding lake-side: bugs, bugs, and more bugs. Bug bites. Bugs buzzing.
- Outdoor wedding in a public park: heat, humidity, bugs, confusing parking, tourists, sketchy bathrooms or worse: port-o-potties.
- Outdoor weddings in the early spring or fall, in the Northeastern part of the US: cold. Hypothermia becomes the concern, instead of heat stroke or fainting. Nobody wants to show up at a wedding in their thickest winter gear, so they wear clothing unsuited to the cold. The guests have it hardest because they are just sitting there the whole time, whereas the bridal party at least gets to walk and stand up. Brides never want to compromise their dress, so they stand in the chill, shaking, shivering, and freezing, just to look good in photos. Mankind worked really hard to design indoor wedding spaces; use them. What's the point of coming up with a unique, meaningful ceremony that nobody enjoys because they are intensely physically uncomfortable?

Some people get lucky and have comfortable, lovely outdoor weddings. I'm sure many people reading this book will have stories of their perfect outdoor wedding where everyone was comfortable or lied to them about being comfortable. That's great, and I am very happy for these people. My point in bringing up this horror-story caution is that I've been a celebrant at so many uncomfortable outdoor weddings, I'm amazed the word hasn't gotten out that they are a possibility.

Why risk it? Make sure you have a comfortable, nearby, sheltered area ready to be your Plan B.

OPEN BAR: These two words are all you need to remember when planning your cocktail hour. Once the ceremony is over, your guests gravitate toward the bar like moths to flames or Steven Soderbergh to heist films. Guests who drink are thrilled at the prospect of free drinks, guests who don't drink try drinking because hey, it's free, and guests who shouldn't drink do drink because everybody else is drinking. People fall off wagons. People cannonball off wagons into wading pools. Deciding to have an open bar is like deciding to have Baz Luhrmann choreograph all the dance numbers for the reception. Open bars are an invitation to lowered inhibitions, revelry, and celebration.

When a guest orders a drink and has to fork over cash . . . oy vey. The message guests take from a cash bar is 'Not only do we not care how much our wedding has already cost you, but your philosophy of alcohol as a solution is your problem. We'd prefer that you remain sober and respectful as we celebrate our perfect love the way it was always intended to be celebrated: like butlers at a funeral. Sincerely, Mr. and Mrs. Stuffypants Killjoy.'

♥

PACHELBEL'S "CANON IN D": Pachelbel's "Canon in D" is "The Star-Spangled Banner" of weddings. Johnny "Tight-Knickers" Pachelbel, or whatever his name was, wrote this piece of music about his camera one day in Germany after ingesting a plate of bratwurst. Most people don't know that the piece is supposed to be played three times as fast with a reggae beat. The version of Pachelbel's "Canon" that most people know is a dirge so beautiful, angels swoon when they hear it. Mothers begin crying as soon as they hear the opening chords. It is known among wedding pros as "Taco Bell's Canon" (Yo Quiero Pachelbel). Also, some people feel the need to specify it as "Canon *in D*," although I've never heard it described as being in any other key. Would "Canon in G" be better? Is G a key? I'm not a musician. I mean, maybe we should give "Canon in Q" a try.

PEOPLE WHO CAN PERFORM YOUR WEDDING CERE-MONY AND MAKE YOU LEGALLY MARRIED: (See: CERTI-FIED LIFE-CYCLE CELEBRANT®, FRIEND, JUDGE, OFFICIANT, PRIEST, IMAN, RABBI, SHIP'S CAPTAIN)

PETS: Aren't pets adorable? Well, yours are. Some people like to include their pets in the wedding ceremony. (Same people who take them on airplanes?) Why? Some college kid somewhere must have written a thesis paper about this, and if they haven't, what are they waiting for? We don't have time to delve into the psychology of people who bring pets to ceremonies. (He's my plus-woof.)

Some couples love pets, and that's cool. Some couples use a co-owned pet as a sneak preview of how each other will be as a parent of a human being. For example, if their pet Pug Mr. Pugly can live for several years, get accepted into the University of Alabama and make them proud, maybe a human baby they produce will do just as well. If the couple has a hard time maintaining any pet longer than a few weeks and spends a lot of time flushing dead pets down the toilet even when they're not fish, perhaps that does not bode well for the potential life span of any human baby they create.

Some couples know that they can't have children and others know they don't want to have children, so the pet they co-own becomes their surrogate child. The pet features in their engagement photos and their wedding registry. The pet no doubt needs to be part of the ceremony.

Many couples want to have their pets attend the wedding, but their venue denies them this joy because the venue does not allow pets. A great solution for couples is to use photographs and the local Staples store to create life-sized cardboard cutouts of their pets, so they can be placed at significant spots during the ceremony. Later, at cocktail hour and the reception, people can include the cutouts in fun photos.

Come to think of it, couples can do the same with family members who can't make it to the ceremony. Or with celebrities they wish were at their ceremony.

PHOTOGRAPHERS: Photographers are people who see more with one eye than most people do with two. Wedding days have become day-long photo sessions. Wedding ceremonies are recorded by multiple photo and video professionals. Even in the most dramatic moments, with the bride making a dramatic entrance and walking up the artfully decorated aisle, there's a photographer kneeling between her and the groom, trying to capture the look on her face as she walks up the aisle. Then the photographer steps in front of the bride's family, blocking their view of the father giving the bride away. Occasionally a photographer will step close to the couple as they exchange rings, trying to get a close-up view of the hands as the rings slip along their fingers.

The photographers who get this close, who are this obtrusive, are bad photographers. These are photographers who don't know how to use a zoom lens.

Most professional wedding photographers are unobtrusive. Some of them are so subtle, they could dress like Lady Gaga and you still would have no idea they are there.

Ideally, photographers work in teams. This way, they have help setting up lighting equipment and they can split up to capture moments in multiple rooms or the same moments from different angles.

The best photographers will capture moments nobody could ever foresee: the wistful look in a parent's eye, a child overcome with giggles, a groomsman making out with your cousin in the coat-check room. These are moments you won't want to miss.

I kid, but some of my best friends are wedding photographers. Good ones will see what you can't see and capture it for you. Get a good photographer.

PHOTO SHOOT: If we all had better memories, we wouldn't need photos to remember things, but just like teenagers who lie and community theater productions of *Annie*, photos are here to stay.

With good reason: what would Pinterest be without photos? Imagine if Pinterest was just a bunch of things people tried to describe with words. (A wooden ampersand! A cloud that looks like Delaware! A baby stuck to a wall with Velcro!) Photos make magazines more readable, scrapbooks more colorful, blackmail more lucrative.

Couples want photographs of the venue, the venue's lawn, and the venue's giant entrance sign. They want photos of the limousine that drops off the bridal party, the driver of the limo, the driver of the limo posing seductively on the hood. They want photos of the welcome table, the guest book, the basket of mints in the men's room. They want photos of the family photos, some of which are photos of family photos at other weddings. They want photos of the ceremony space before and after the florists work their magic. They want close-ups of vines and flowers and topiary. They want views from the roof and from ankle-level. They want photos of the chairs and those standing candle-holder things that people put at the row entrances if they are masochists. They want photos of the dining tables, the centerpieces, the dance floor, the band, the band's equipment and instruments. They want photos of guests arriving, sitting down, standing up, eating, drinking, and dancing.

They want posed photos of family members in various combinations. Here are some ideas to help you and your photogs have the Best. Photo Session. Ever.

Once you've shot the usual combination of the whole family, men, women, bride's family, groom's family, friends . . .

Mix it up. Crank some music, give them some drinks, get them dancing. Whether they're doing their own groove, a synchronized Macarena, a whip/nae-nae, an electric slide, or a combination of all these dances (an Electric Macanae-nae) these will be awesome photos. Here are some ideas with corresponding music ideas.

- Maybe some grinding for all the couples (Marvin Gaye)
- Get the grandmas decked out in bling and have them do some gangsta posing (Jay-Z)
- Manic freestyle rocking for the ring bearer and flower girl (Green Day)
- A Venetian masquerade, with those masques on sticks (Vitamin String Ensemble)
- Scarves (Fleetwood Mac)
- Top hats and canes (Duke Ellington)
- Best Man in the Philly Fanatic costume (David Lee Roth solo work)
- Glasses with mustaches and noses (Bruno Mars)
- Clown noses (Insane Clown Posse)
- Elton John-like jackets (Elton John)
- Lady Gaga-like outfits (Lady Gaga)
- Enormous shoes (Justin Timberlake)
- Is there a trampoline nearby? Let's use it. (Katy Perry)
- Get everyone to jump rope as one! (Beyoncé)
- How about a bed of hot coals? (Mighty Mighty Bosstones)

In other words, try *anything* other than just having everyone stand there struggling to smile.

Mix up the location. Do you have access to a golf course? Just think of the sand trap photo ops! (They look like little beaches!)

Is there a street nearby with no traffic on it? (Make family members walk across the street, one of them barefoot, like the cover of the Beatles' *Abbey Road*.) Do you have access to a rooftop? What about a meat locker? A skating rink? A brewery? A wine cellar? What about an S&M red room or a Pilates studio (if you can tell the difference)? Use any space you can to create something memorable.

The only thing to avoid is getting anybody injured doing some kind of contortion beyond their scope, which is why I am not mentioning the idea of a cheerleader-style family pyramid or a grandmothers-only trust-fall.

PINTEREST: The photo-sharing site where complete strangers give couples ideas and/or make them feel that they are in an inferior creative sphere. Pinterest is a great place to brainstorm wedding ideas. You can sort of attend weddings around the world on Pinterest. I don't have a sponsorship from Pinterest (yet!) but I strongly suggest you allow your mind to absorb thousands of wedding photos until your mind blends as one with the site; then, if nothing else, you will know what your wedding planner's brain is like.

PLAN B: If you are planning on having an outdoor wedding, you should also have an indoor (or at least sheltered) plan B to which you can turn in the event of inclement weather. Imagine having all your dressed-up guests standing around in the rain as you try to decide where to send all of them. Picture the water ruining your dress, makeup running down your face and the Bridesmaids' faces, hair flattened, the chill of water dripping down your spine, the empty clarity that you have made a terrible error in judgment by not heeding this book's warnings about outdoor weddings. Picture the looks on your family's faces as they glare at you, waiting for instructions, wind whipping their hearing aids out of their ears, chairs overturning in the gale, children crying, old women trying to run but collapsing when their hips snap. Picture it! If you don't have an indoor or sheltered plan B, this will come true!!! (Evil Empire Music)

PLANNING: Probably the easiest part of the whole process.

Kidding! Planning is such a huge part of a wedding, there is a whole type of professional dedicated to it: your Mom. Kidding! Sort of. Moms sort of become wedding planners the moment they become moms. This is why so many mothers see their baby for the first time, squeeze their husband's arm, and command, 'Hire a caterer.'

Here is all you have to plan—it's really quite a short list, and I'm sure that as soon as you read it, which won't take long, you will relax about the whole planning process—ready? Okay, here is *all* you have to plan:

- who to marry
- when to marry
- where to marry
- whom to invite
- what to feed them
- where to seat everyone for the reception dinner
- when to have your rehearsal
- when to have your rehearsal dinner
- where to have your rehearsal dinner
- where to have your day-after brunch
- which vendors to hire
- what to wear
- what rings you'll give each other
- where guests will stay
- where guests will park
- what guests will do while they're in town

- how to make the wedding ceremony unique
- how guests will get from the ceremony to cocktail hour
- how to pay for the whole thing
- how to get your parents to pay for the whole thing
- dozens of other miscellaneous things that pop up on the design end of things

See? Easy!

P R I E S T : A leader who may perform the sacred rites and rituals of their religion; for example, a wedding ceremony. Many priests will be reluctant to perform a wedding ceremony outside of a church because rules is rules.

P R O P O S A L : A marriage proposal is just a simple question that happens to have lifelong consequences for multiple people (you, your partner, and anybody involved in the office pool on when you'll get engaged). That said, it's the kind of question that shouldn't be asked until the asker is sure that the answer is a foregone conclusion, with the question being a mere formality. Just as trial lawyers only ask questions to which they know the answers, by the time the proposer is proposing, he or she should really know what the answer will be, because the person being asked has already indicated that the question should be asked. Yeah, it's complicated. In fact, it's a four-part process:

- Part One: The Supposal
- Part Deux: Parental Permission
- Part Three: Finger Measuring/Ring Shopping
- Part D: Actual Proposal

Part One: Usually, the proposee knows a proposal is coming because she and her boyfriend have had an oblique, no-obligations, preliminary conversation about getting married, something I call "The Supposal."

"Suppose we got married? Do you suppose that might be a good idea?"

"Sure, I suppose so."

So the Supposal ™© precedes the proposal.

Part Deux, Parental Permission: After The Supposal, in traditional proposals, the groom asks the father of the bride for permission to marry his daughter. Once the groom obtains the dad's permission, he concocts his big proposal plan. (Why shouldn't the proposer have to ask the mother of the bride for her permission too? Doesn't the wife make all the decisions in the marriage anyway? We all know she does.)

I would love to see this tradition upended: I'd love it if the woman would have to ask permission from the groom's parents too—fair is fair, plus, just think how much more assured the couple could feel knowing that *four* parents approve versus only *two*? Yeah. Think about that.

Same-sex couples have struggled with the notion of "permission" for long enough—they have every right to adopt, reject, or redefine this tradition of permission seeking. On the one hand, perhaps both halves of any couple should ask the other half's parents for permission; on the other hand, if marriage really is between two people—not four, not six—who says anyone needs parental permission, or any permission at all? That said, since marriage remains the only institution that joins families together (and these days our world can use all the harmony it can find), it would behoove anyone seeking to get married to have both families behind their decision.

If the couple asks one set of parents and gets a resounding "no," then asks the other set of parents and gets a second resounding "no," then asks friends, co-workers, and other family members for their opinions, and every which way they turn they find hesitation, doubt, subject-changing, sudden gaps in cell phone reception, and outright negative responses, it may be time to take a step back and reconsider things. Even if half of the people asked say "no" and the other half says "yes," couples might want to reconvene at the old drawing board. Seeking permission is another way of seeking validation and reassurance. Marriage is the relationship Autobahn: when a couple is traveling at 120 miles per hour, they really ought to have miles of green lights awaiting them.

Chris, are you a feminist?
I prefer "genius sociological innovator."

Part Three: Finger Measuring/Ring Shopping: Proposers need to accept this basic fact: the proposal itself *will not and should not ever be a complete surprise*, in that the proposee does not have any idea that the proposer wants to marry them. That scenario is both not fair and totally goes against protocol. So, don't worry proposers, if you need to straight-up ask your girlfriend/ partner what her ring size is and if she has any kind of preference for ring size/outlandishness/diamond requirement. This is totally normal and totally respectful of the protocol of this four-part process. *The proposal itself should be a surprise* and it still can be: just because they know you're going to propose doesn't mean they know *how* or *when* you will propose.

Part D: Actual Proposal: Traditionally, men ask women to marry them, and all the pressure is on them to come up with something memorable. (In same-sex couples, the rules are less defined because these couples have very little history upon which to call. Either half of the couple, or both members of the couple, may propose. Why can't it be this way with opposite-sex couples? That was a trick question: it can, but tradition has a vice-grip on our collective psyche.)

Surprise may be the cornerstone of a story-worthy proposal, but knowing one's audience is key. If a man asks his incredibly shy wallflower-standing-behind-another-wallflower girlfriend to marry him by putting them on the jumbotron at a sports event, thus putting her on the spot in front of thousands of people in the stadium, she should say no, then reconnect with the guitar player poet she dated sophomore year of college and then lost touch with when he transferred to Wesleyan. If his girlfriend is an outgoing, exuberant fellow sports nut who previously dated most of his fellow football teammates, great! This is a great idea in that scenario. If the girlfriend is incredibly shy, he should propose to her at home, in the dark, with the shades drawn, via text message.

Proposals are unique to each couple. Proposals can be public and elaborate, private and simple, private and elaborate, public and simple. These days, men make videos of their relationship, rent screen time in movie theaters, lie to their girlfriends about them seeing a private screening, then watch as the girlfriend cries throughout the video they spent a fortune producing with a buddy and some guy his buddy knows. (Just . . . don't ask questions about the buddy.)

Men hire skywriters, clandestine photographers, and flash-mobs. Men try to outdo each other's proposals, and they don't even know each other! Men are competing against total strangers with their proposals just so their girlfriend can't complain that they didn't make an effort.

Okay, not all men go crazy with their proposals, but all of them try to incorporate surprise. The plan does not always work. Benches with sunset views are pummeled by rainstorms. Girlfriends have too much wine early in the dinner so by the time the proposal happens the girl is sauced. A private moment gets ruined by clueless strangers. Birds poop at just the wrong moment.

Timing is important: a lot of proposals happen in the days preceding the holidays, so people can show off their news to gathered relatives. They happen in ordinary moments when nothing extraordinary is going on. They happen at the beginning of a vacation so couples can spend the week celebrating something amazing; they happen at the end of vacations to make the trip home exciting.

There is an urgency these days to capture the proposal moment on camera and video. This necessitates co-conspirators, planning, timing, and strategy. As an older person who did not record his own proposal, I recommend only recording the moment *in your own mind.* I can go back to the moment I proposed to my wife in the baggage claim area at McCarren Airport in Las Vegas anytime I want, remember exactly what she was wearing, exactly what I was feeling, and the elation as she jumped into my arms and I spun her round and round. No piece of recording equipment other than my heart could possibly capture the elation I'd never felt before and have never felt since.* We have no photos of the moment, no video, nothing. Doesn't matter. It's right there in my head and hers.

If you need examples of how other proposals went down, head over to HowHeAsked.com, where they curate such things.

Every proposal boils down to one human being asking another human being to share their lives with them. A proposal is just a question the way the big bang was just an explosion. (Nobody has actual photos of the big bang but we're all most impressed by it.)

*The Red Sox winning the World Series in 2004 came close.

♥

QUARREL: A quarrel is like an argument, only both of you are in the eighteenth century.

Quarrels are totally normal. Couples who say they don't quarrel are either lying, telling the truth but have a huge quarrel coming their way, or prefer to use the word argue.

QUESTIONNAIRE: A questionnaire is an opportunity for the couple to write about themselves so that the person marrying them knows them better. Who doesn't enjoy being asked about themselves? Well, criminals, probably. Other than criminals, most people enjoy regaling others about their relationship and how much they mean to each other. We are ego-driven life-forms in a social media–saturated world.

A questionnaire full of anecdotes about your relationship is the most useful thing you can give your wedding officiant (other than money), especially if you've been honest, forthcoming and generous with your personal facts. Don't blow off the questionnaire. Do it. It's critical to making a meaningful ceremony.

The only thing that short-circuits questionnaires are clichés: phrases like, "he's my everything," "she means the world to me," and "he's my rock" pop up in questionnaire responses all the time. They're pretty useless. You can do better. You can't be someone's rock. Only rocks are rocks, only Ford Trucks are "like a rock." And only Dwayne "The Rock" Johnson and Alcatraz the prison are The Rock.

Short answers don't help much either: "We met at work." "We met through mutual friends." "We met on a Friday." These all may be factual, but they are also vague and boring. Responses like this require follow-up and who's got the time?

(See also Questions for Couples on page 139)

♥

RABBI: A teacher of the Torah; an interpreter of Jewish law. For a wedding that takes place in a Jewish temple, couples will need a Rabbi to perform the wedding ceremony. Many Rabbis are reluctant to perform a wedding outside a temple, and certainly for any couple who may be interdenominational, because rules is rules.

READINGS: Passages from novels, poems, songs, encyclopedias, user's manuals, soap opera transcripts, etc. that say something meaningful about love, marriage and/or the couple getting married.

If you want someone to do a reading during your wedding ceremony, choose someone who can actually speak well in public and enjoys doing so, otherwise the reading becomes a regrettable waste of time, like a grade-school production of *The Iceman Cometh*.

REASONS TO GET MARRIED: Why get married? The simplest and most complicated answer is love.

Love is a many-splendored mystery, impossible to understand how it works or to live without, like a smartphone: people want to find someone who feels comfortable in their hands, whose apps are easy to use and who will be responsive to their touch. They want someone who seems to know what they want even before they do. They want someone who will grow and change and update themselves with new, useful, exciting, and more efficient functions. They want someone they can afford to be with, who recharges when they plug them in and who looks good with very little to cover them.

While love plays a major role in relationships, the decision to marry can be influenced by several life factors. Like most big life decisions, the most common motivators are sex, money, and taxes. As fascinating as money and taxes are, let's begin with sex. (Okay!)

Sex: Both men and women find great comfort in knowing that they are their partner's only sex partner currently, with currently being from this day forward. It's not easy to find someone with whom you would like to have exclusive sex for the rest of your life. I mean, there are tons of attractive people out there. How do you choose just one? And why on earth would anyone choose you? Sexual compatibility is a tricky thing to find, a complicated mixture of trust, love, and hunger that other experts would be better at explaining, plus, I'm trying to keep things clean here. Sure, the virgins out there might think that virgins marrying virgins is the optimal way to go, but what do virgins know? See? Even Grandma is horrified at that notion and believe me, Grandma is no virgin. I'd love to be romantic and say that virgins marrying virgins is a great idea, but I'd say it in a high-pitched reluctant voice while wearing my skeptic face. (I hope to demonstrate this face on TV one day.) Put another way, when you go to a restaurant, and you shell out $28 to have chicken parmesan for the first time or thirtieth time, do you hope that this is the first time the chef has prepared chicken parmesan, or would it be better if he'd made chicken parmesan for several people before you walked in the door? (And how many = several?)

Money: Money is obviously a big issue. I've seen every iteration of the comparison of finances: he doesn't have money, but she does; she doesn't have money, but he does; neither of them has money, but their parents do; their parents have no money, but they do. In the old days, marriages were a financial arrangement, and brides were just part of a bigger deal which often included real estate, oxen, and a third-round draft pick. These days, the financial aspect of a wedding union is gauche to talk about but everyone knows it's there. Let's just say that just as settlers seek out water sources, and rivers seek the ocean, less money seeks out more money.

Taxes: Taxes are a fact of life, like death and Jon Stewart cameos on *Colbert*. Taxes are the least sexy reason for getting married, but taxes are, after all, representative of and effecting of money. There are something like 1,963 benefits that a pair of spouses have that a pair of non-spouses do not. Or that may be the number of assists Wayne Gretzky had in his career. I'm not great with statistics. Point is, there are so many potential tax benefits for married couples that I wonder why people don't just get married legally as soon as they can, even before they finish planning their gigantic wedding. (See also ELOPEMENTS) (It's staggering to think that same-sex couples have been denied these benefits all these years just because their love somehow makes certain people uncomfortable even though the couple's love has absolutely nothing to do with anybody but them.)

Consult your tax accountant for specifics, but in the meantime, here are some generalities!

You might save a bunch of money if you file jointly! You also might not! If you don't get married, you definitely won't. Chances are, your financial situations are different from each other's. Depending on the dynamic of this see-saw tilt, being married might save you some money. The scenario of a rock star married to a school teacher may bring tax bennies; the scenario of two married rock stars may bring tax burdens. Most couples' scenarios are probably somewhere between these two scenarios. Consult your tax accountant, tea leaves and/or palm reader.

Prenuptial Agreement Benefits: If the couple makes very different amounts of money, a prenup will protect the poorer one; it's like socialism for your relationship!

IRA Benefits: If you're married and you invest in a retirement account, both of you can benefit from this account, no matter which one of you is doing the heavy-contributing!

Legal Decision-Making Benefits: If your spouse is incapacitated by injury, sickness or dementia, you can sit behind the desk, put your feet up, light a cigar and call the shots! Buy! Sell! Take Ned out of the will!

Health Insurance Benefits: If only one of you has a job that provides health care, that's fine, your spouse can still receive health care even though he can't find a job! You get to have both health care *and* the moral upper hand because you provide the health care. The non-health-care-providing spouse has to keep his or her mouth shut during other arguments because when the dust settles, the one who provides the health care is clearly the more valuable and therefore the one who is probably right about whatever old thing you're arguing (or quarreling) about.

Sick-Leave Benefits: If your spouse is sick or in the hospital, and you need to miss work to be with your spouse, you can do that if you're married and be compensated for it! This benefit does not do anything for you if you are simply sick *of* your spouse. In that case, simply leave. If you are stumped for ways to leave, consult Paul Simon's song "50 Ways to Leave Your Lover."

Next-of-Kin for Hospital Visits: If your spouse is sick or dying or both, in the hospital, you can visit your spouse in the hospital for long nights spent agonizing over the inevitability of entropy, *and* you can finish the Jell-O that they probably won't.

Sue for Wrongful-Death of Spouse: If your spouse dies, wrongfully, you can sue the hospital or whoever wrongfully death-ed your spouse for lots of money, and when you win, the two of you can . . . whoops, sorry. Okay, silver lining: If you win, you can sleep on a bed of cash, alone, or with your next spouse, it's really up to you at that point. Unless you believe in ghosts. Or even then. What is your ghost spouse gonna do, other than drive you crazy by rattling chains and playing old songs by *The Smiths?* (How soon *is* now?)

Inheritance with No Tax Penalty: It's true, a spouse can inherit the other spouse's stuff and not pay any taxes on it! One more reason to be kind to each other. So many of these benefits have to do with one spouse dying, which explains a lot of episodes of *Dateline.*

Social Security Benefits: If one of you dies, the living one can receive the dead one's social security benefits! If that's not a great reason to make that vow about till-death-do-us-part, I don't know what is! If both of you die, you won't care about this.

Other Reasons to Get Married: Beyond these big motivating factors for people to get married are other, more complicated external societal and internal neurobiological factors.

Outside pressure: Some people get married because their parents want them to.

Some people get married because their parents *don't* want them to.

Most often, it's young people who let their parents pressure them into getting married. "What are you waiting for?" they may ask. "You aren't getting any younger," they may cajole in a Jamaican accent. "It's not like you've got a parade of gentleman callers lined up outside your door." they may remind you in a southern accent. "I may die tomorrow," they may threaten in an Irish accent while clutching their heart. "Do you want your poor mother to die without seeing her only daughter get married? Is that what you want?"

Many parents want couples to get married because they want to have grandchildren, which is a terrible reason to get married (and a terrible reason to have sex). Nobody should get married just because their parents want them to have children. Don't get me started.

Psychological Benefits: Having a person who loves you around is great for your emotional health. A spouse can make sure you experience happiness, even if that means they occasionally make you miserable. They only make you miserable so you can appreciate the delightful contrast of feeling happy. It's the Yin/Yang thing.

Increased serotonin levels: Serotonin is one of the body's natural antidepressants. When someone makes you happy, your brain releases serotonin, the happy drug that keeps your glasses rose-colored. Your spouse should make you happier than anyone because he or she has the most access to you.

Less chance of developing depression: According to science, spouses are less likely to develop depression. (Obviously, science has never been married. *Hey-ohhhhh!*)

While spouses may depress each other, the way to look on the bright side is that they often serve as a valuable check-and-balance, keeping each other up-to-date on world events, correcting each other if necessary, questioning each other to make sure they can see all sides of an issue, serving as honest mirrors so they won't wear that horrible outdated jacket to the Wilsons', popping the balloon of their flawed argument privately at home so the spouse won't be embarrassed when their friends pop it in public, later on, at the holiday party. Being a spouse keeps you mentally involved and active. This is why one spouse often passes away soon after the first spouse does—this also happens because the spouse's ghost drives them crazy, rattling chains and playing old albums by *The Smiths*.

Longevity: Being (happily) married can keep you alive longer, according to medical people who research such things. Remaining unhappily married may make you *feel* as if you have been alive longer than you have.

Whatever motivates you to get married, always remember that it's *your* wedding, not *their* wedding, whoever *they* may be. Forgetting this fact is how people get hurt, and how ceremonial spaces get draped in yellow police tape.

R E C E S S I O N A L : This is the part at the end of the ceremony where the bridal party and immediate family members leave the ceremonial space in order to have first dibs at cocktail hour drinks.

R E G I S T R Y : Registries are the Amazon wish list of couplehood. They take the guesswork out of giving the couple a gift. Registries are also the product of big assumptions of etiquette. Any couple getting married *probably* has friends and family members; these friends and family members *probably* want to buy them a gift, (and, per etiquette, are expected to do so) and instead of the couple receiving a bunch of stuff they don't need or want, a registry clearly outlines what they want and need (for example this book, to give to friends) for their future life together.

Couples with a conscience can request that in lieu of gifts, or in addition to gifts, guests contribute to a worthy charity like Team Rubicon, the Natural Resources Defense Council, the Trevor Project, Planned Parenthood, the American Civil Liberties Union, the Anti-Defamation League or any other organization towards which John Oliver directs our attention on *Last Week Tonight*.

REHEARSAL: Rehearsals are a chance for your bridal party to come together and learn what is expected of them during the wedding ceremony. Rehearsals can be as brief as ten to fifteen minutes or can take up an hour, depending on how complicated your ceremony is and how long your bridal party's attention spans may be. Rehearsals often happen the night before the wedding, because some brides and grooms don't want to see each other on the wedding day until the ceremony. Also, some couples are worried that a 'rehearsal dinner' wouldn't be the same without the rehearsal part. Rehearsals can also happen on the day of the wedding. Even if your rehearsal is super-casual, have a rehearsal. If your ceremony involves music, choreography, cooperation, timing, effects, gags, anything at all...definitely have a rehearsal.

REHEARSAL DINNER: The meal that happens after your rehearsal. Later, there may be "rehearsal drinking," "rehearsal movie-going," or "rehearsal karaoke." All of this happens after rehearsal and depends on what you've got going on that night. It's a great excuse for your family and friends to get together the night before the wedding. You don't even really have to have a rehearsal before the rehearsal dinner. You can just pretend that you are rehearsing having a good time.

RING BEAR: A Ring Bearer wearing a big bear head. This is only good for English-speaking countries; other countries need to find their own puns.

(Racy alternate use: if you have a large, hairy gay man in your group, he too can be a Ring Bear. More subtle and less adorable, maybe, but given the right crowd, golden.)

RING WARMING: A ring warming is an inclusive ritual that can involve as many or as few guests as the couple wishes. The idea is that the guests send good wishes, prayers, and thoughts into the rings, imbuing the rings with positive energy. This allows everyone to feel as if they have contributed something spiritual to the couple. It's a lovely ritual that belongs to no singular religion, culture or geographic region. It's universal, holistic, and completely free.

Options for ring warmings:

- The rings are passed around (usually in a bag, where they are tied together) to every guest, row by row, at the beginning of the ceremony, so every guest gets to actually hold the rings for a moment. Ushers or bridal party members make sure the rings get to everyone and make their way, eventually, back to the best man or whoever is responsible for holding the rings. This is unobtrusive and can happen while the ceremony is underway.

- Another option is to have the rings displayed on a table, past which every guest must walk to get to their seats. The guests can pause at the table, wish good thoughts upon the rings, and then take their seats. Once all that is done, an usher or bridal party member makes sure the rings get to whoever is responsible for holding them. Couples can decorate this table to explain the ring warming, to share facts about the rings, and to thank all the guests for being such an important part of their big day.

- Another way is to select certain family members—parents, perhaps, or just dads, or just moms, to come up at a significant moment to bless the rings either silently or with a vocalized prayer or thoughts.

(Couples can also place the rings in a microwave and cook them on high for a minute or so—once the microwave catches fire and explodes, the rings and everything around them will be quite warm. This is more of a Jason Bourne ring warming.)

(See also RITUALS)

R I N G S : Rings are the round things you see on married men and women's ring fingers (left hand: the finger that is not your pinky finger, your middle finger, your index finger or your thumb finger). (Just to be absolutely clear: not the finger you extend when drinking champagne, not the finger you use to flip off other drivers, not the finger you use to get the waiter's attention, not the finger you use to hitchhike.)

If you see a wedding ring on someone's finger, don't flirt with them! Marriage is hard enough without hotties like yourself distracting people from the serious work of being a good spouse. If they are wearing a wedding band and are flirting with you, their marriage is on the rocks; then it's up to you whether you'd like to be involved in a romantic tragedy free-fall. Sure: maybe they made a mistake, maybe they're meant to be with you. Maybe they are a horrible person. In any case, now you know what a ring is.

Rings are both symbolic and practical. The symbolism comes from the shape: they are round, like the letter O and hula hoops. The symbolism of all round things is pretty good: they don't begin or end anywhere. Rings represent what has been and what will always be. You can't get that kind of top-grade symbolism from a hexagon, and triangles have other connotations. Rings are symbolic of the ever-regenerating love that exists between the couple. Plus, they fit easily on the finger, unlike hula hoops.

Engagement rings are usually expensive. No man wants to give his wife a cheap ring, even if she told you she would marry you even if you gave her an onion ring. (Still not sure if my wife was kidding.) Wedding rings are less expensive and showy than engagement rings, because by the time the couple buys the wedding rings they have spent their life savings on the other aspects of their wedding.

RISKY IDEAS: Getting married. Getting married outdoors. Getting married to Tom Cruise. Skydiving. Careers in figure skating. Juggling chainsaws. The stock market. Machiavellian dictatorship. Tiramisu.

RITUALS: Rituals in wedding ceremonies are acted-out metaphors. The lighting of Unity Candles, the filling of Unity Sand, sharing wine, ring warming, invoking the four directions (Uptown, Downtown, East Side, West Side), blessing stones, tying the knot (a.k.a. Handfasting), memory boxes, all of these things are rituals in wedding ceremonies.

The basic idea is to represent the metaphorical aspect of two lives intermingling in a visible way that will benefit the wedding ritual industry.

Rituals are great for wedding guests who don't quite get the big picture of what's happening or who don't understand the same language that the officiant is speaking. Rituals are great for photos: candles are always pretty, the mixed sand can make beautiful designs, and two hands joined by a thick rope, scarf, or hockey skate laces invoke the bond of bondage.

(See also BREAKING OF THE GLASS; HANDFASTING; JUMPING THE BROOM; KNOT, TYING THE; MEMORY BOXES; SAND; UNITY CANDLE; UNITY RITUAL)

RSVP: RSVP is an acronym for *répondez, s'il vous plait*. Translated into English, this means, 'are you coming or what?'

Not to be fussy, but if they really felt you were close and important to them, they'd use the familiar *te* instead of *vous*. (Or as they say, *tutoyer*.) RSVPs would be RSTPs and more people would R. (If you took twelve years of French for no reason, you'd be opportunistically pretentious too.)

RUNNER: The runner is that long white cloth that runs from the entrance area all the way up the aisle to the ceremonial matrimonial space. It looks great in pictures, but in practice, it can be a disaster. Runners are often made out of the kind of flimsy wafer-thin material that Grasshopper (played by David Carradine) had to walk across in *Kung Fu*. They're sometimes so flimsy (HOW...

FLIMSY...ARE THEY?) staff members have to tape them down, which they often can't do until right before the bridal party enters, which means that just when the event you've been planning for a year is about to begin, all anyone notices are staff members down on their hands and knees ripping duct tape off a roll and hastily securing the runner to the carpet, cement, marble, bricks, or even grass, depending on the venue. One of the people bending over will have plumber-butt, and sarcastic family members will reach for a nickel to put in the coin slot. And even if the staff members do tape down the runner, the first one or two people to step on the runner with a high-heeled shoe will likely rip a hole in it anyway. So, by the time the bride and her father enter, the thing is ripped and flopping in the breeze like an albino wacky-wavy-inflatable-arms guy.

 Instead of a traditional runner, use a water slide.

RUSTIC: Rustic is more than just a classy way to describe something that could give you tetanus. Rustic is a useful homonymic. Repurposed warehouse spaces are rustic. Barns are rustic. Nick Nolte is rustic.

Rustic is usually a word used to describe casual, barn-ish or warehouse-ish wedding venues. Rustic describes both the space and its vibe. A rustic wedding implies informality, down-home warmth, blue-collar simplicity, the close proximity of horses, vineyards, farmers, organic vegetables, and staffers with visible tattoos. A rustic wedding evokes images of brides in cowboy boots, grooms in suspenders and bow ties, and groomsmen who seem too young to have such thick beards. Rustic venues showcase distressed wood and rebar. Rustic weddings promise barbecue at the reception, mason jars of craft beer, and live bands that specialize in Dixie music.

♥

SAME-SEX WEDDING: I'm so happy for the same-sex couples of the world who can now marry legally. If you are an opposite-sex couple and you are having a difficult time getting psyched about your wedding, think for a minute that millions of people who love each other and are committed to each other with all the purpose anyone could ever ask for were, for eons, prohibited from marrying for no good reason. Look to same-sex couples for inspiration. Same-sex wedding ceremonies are the most moving, meaningful, heartfelt, joyous, and creative ones I've ever been honored to officiate. Matching outfits, couples entering together, heartfelt vows, bucking tradition at every turn, because really, what tradition could they have? Same-sex couples appreciate the act of joining together in matrimony, and they reflect this appreciation in every aspect of their ceremony. Pure happiness is beautiful to behold.

S A N D : The stuff that gets *everywhere* when you play on a beach with no pants on. Also a substance incorporated into unity rituals because sand can be different colors and anything that can be different colors can also create art. Note that when the sand representing one half the couple and the sand representing the other half of the couple enter the unity sand vial, they do not mix to form a new color; they compromise around each other until they make something as haphazard, yet beautiful, as a fractal. How's that for symbolism? (Sound of reader looking up "fractal.")

(See also RITUALS)

S A V E - T H E - D AT E : A save-the-date is like an invitation but not an invitation. It is merely a request not to book anything else on a certain day while also conveying the message "We haven't gotten around to finalizing our invitations but until we do please do not book anything else that Saturday night." It's sort of like texting someone that you're about to send them an email.

S E A S O N S : Vivaldi wrote music about the four seasons because he loved the hotel. Mother Nature has no idea that we have official days to switch over the seasons. No idea. She doesn't even know that we've decided that there are four of them. Or who Vivaldi is.

Winter: Venue prices are lower in winter, so some couples choose to get married during this, the coldest season. Snow makes for pretty backdrops for pictures. Family and friends have fewer social obligations during winter, so they are more likely to show up. Nobody is going to complain about the heat, and you only have to wait until 4:30 p.m. for sunset. Winter has a lot going for it, especially if you are winter people. Probably not the best time of year for an outdoor wedding. Mother Nature is pretty much swathed in flannel and turtlenecks this time of year.

Spring: Ahh, spring, the lovely season right after winter that often still feels like winter. Early spring can still bring snow. Venue prices sneak up. April showers bring May flowers, and *Mayflowers* bring pilgrims. Rain loves spring. Rain takes its spring break during spring. Spring, for rain, is like Burning Man, only wet. All of rain's friends are there! Late May is a great time of year for weddings, maybe the best, with ideal weather in between rain storms and early heat waves.

Summer: The hottest season and the most popular for weddings. School teachers pretty much have to wait for summer in order to get married. (Teachers are our most important citizens.) The sun is high, the days are long, and the humidity is brutal. With cool drinks, gorgeous sunsets, mosquitoes, and sweat trickling down your back, summer has a lot going for it: heat stroke, blinding light, fainting spells ... who wouldn't want to get married during the summer, indoors, with air conditioning?

Fall: Fall is the new spring. More and more weddings happen during the fall. Venue prices used to fall in the fall, but when venue managers found out that more people wanted to avoid the crippling heat of summer for their weddings, they kept their prices right in the summer sweet range. Colored leaves, cool breezes, hot cider. Fall may be the perfect time of year to get married unless you are a school teacher with a lot more to worry about. (Teachers are our most important citizens.)

In the world of weddings, there are two distinct seasons: good for weddings (all year, if indoors) and bad for weddings (all year, if outdoors). (Unless you have the luck o' the Irish—or even better luck. The Irish weren't that lucky, historically, if you think about it.)

SHIP'S CAPTAIN: Psych! This is actually a Hollywood-inspired myth. A captain of a ship may solemnize a wedding if he or she is *also* a judge, ordained minister, justice of the peace, or otherwise state-licensed wedding officiant. A captain of a ship may not legally marry a couple solely on the basis of the fact that he or she is the captain of a ship. They can perform ceremonies all they want, as can anyone, but the couple will need someone legitimate to sign their marriage license to make the union legal. (Shipboard wedding ceremonies have become so popular, however, that some cruise lines have taken steps to make sure that their captains may, in fact, solemnize wedding unions. If it is a dream of yours to be married on board a ship by the ship's captain, contact your preferred cruise line to get the facts.)

SIGNATURE DRINK: Create a signature drink of your own, one that represents your relationship. For example, Sammy and Brenda met in Long Island at an Ice-T concert, so their signature drink is an Old Fashioned.

SILVER: Silver represents the twenty-fifth wedding anniversary. The traditional gift is a horse named Silver.

SOMETHING OLD, SOMETHING NEW, SOMETHING BORROWED, SOMETHING BLUE: Tradition has it that by wearing something old (to protect a baby), something new (fresh start), something borrowed (for good luck), and something blue (to protect fidelity), a bride will have good luck on her wedding day. Couples may get creative with interpreting any of these items.

Something old:

- Your grandmother's wedding dress
- Your grandmother's earrings
- Your grandmother's bra

Something new:

- A wedding dress specially tailored to your body
- A pair of shoes designed by your favorite designer
- A Fitbit, so you can see how many calories you burn walking up the aisle

Something borrowed:

- One of your father's monogrammed handkerchiefs, folded into a secret pocket on your dress, upon which you may dab away happy tears
- One of your mother's elaborate necklaces, perhaps the one she wore at her own wedding
- One of your little sister's packets of Listerine strips, because the onions from that morning's omelet keep repeating on you

Something blue:

- Blue nail polish, lovingly applied by your youngest sister, the flower girl, in a tender, bonding moment
- Blue lace from your Italian grandmother's home on the isle of Burano, lovingly wrapped about the handle of your bouquet
- Dr. Scholl's orthopedic inserts, because the heel support really helps your lower back

SPEECHES: At a wedding reception, it is traditional for the father of the bride to do a short speech, and in this day and age, it's more acceptable for the mother of the bride to do a speech too, because, after all, if a woman can vote, why can't she do a speech at her daughter's wedding? This is followed by the best man and maid of honor speeches, in no particular order. Let the best speaker go last.

Father or Mother Speech: Serves to welcome the guests, thank everyone involved, jest at how the relationship with the new son-in-law/daughter-in-law changed over time, welcome him/her to the family, poke fun at their actual son/daughter in a way that will not overly embarrass him/her. End by raising a glass to the happy couple.

Best Man Speech: Serves to further welcome everyone, compliment the bridesmaids, maid of honor, and especially the bride for being beautiful, make light of how she could do much better than the groom she has chosen, then ruthlessly emasculate the groom in front of his friends, family, and new wife. End by raising a glass to the happy couple.

Maid of Honor Speech: Serves to further thank everyone, share touchy-feely anecdote about her relationship with the bride, make everybody cry, compliment the groom, give the groom advice because the MOH knows the bride better than anybody, threaten the groom with explicit details as to what will happen to him if he dares hurt the bride in any way. The best MOH speeches hint that they may have been each other's "experiment" in college. End by raising a glass to the happy couple.

SYMBOLISM: A symbol is anything that represents an idea. A symbol is a substitute for words. A symbol is worth a thousand words, and a picture is worth a thousand words, so a picture of a symbol would be worth, according to my math, a lot of words, which is why photographers charge so much.

Couples can display symbols of their relationship in lots of ways throughout the wedding day: table settings, signs, decorations, even the text of the ceremony can allude to something that has symbolic meaning for the couple. Symbols can be a part of invitations, ceremony programs, bar napkins, matchbooks, welcome bags for guests in hotel rooms, or logos on the couple's wedding website. Symbols can be subtle yet pervasive or acknowledged in overt fashion, depending on the couple, on the symbol and on the effect the couple would like to achieve by sharing a symbol that has meaning for them.

For some couples, the restaurant where they met becomes a symbol of their relationship. A song can be a symbol of their love. An out of the way Hyatt Regency can be a symbol for the early days of their courtship. A burner phone can be a symbol of their deep feelings for each other. A lawyer's business card can be a symbol of the circumstances surrounding their coupling. Symbols can be small things like lockets, cufflinks, or the wall phone they used to speak to each other through the secure window when he visited her in prison. Symbols don't have to be literal placeholders of a moment, time, or feeling; symbols can be absolutely anything that conjures up, for the couple, something meaningful about their relationship. (Like handcuffs or those little tools that IKEA gives you to help assemble a STORJORM.)

♥

TOASTS: Toasts are like speeches, only much shorter. A toast serves only one purpose: to celebrate a noun or nouns.

Examples:

- "To the bride; may the groom be the last thing she settles for."
- "To the happy couple; may the lowest thing in their lives be their expectations."
- "To the happy couple; may the worst thing they do be the last thing the police discover."
- "To the perfect couple; whoever they may be."
- "To the thrill of young love and the comfort of Tylenol."
- "To love; may you find it in the last place you look."
- "To the Kama Sutra; the best reason to do yoga."

TUXEDO: A tuxedo is something a person wears to a black-tie event. The traditional wedding cake topper shows a groom in a tuxedo. This is also the preferred attire of James Bond whenever he enters a casino, hotel, luxury train dining car, or really any establishment after dark. During fierce bouts of insomnia, James Bond wears a tuxedo to the all-night laundry place to wash his other tuxedos.

♥

UMBRELLAS: Are you planning on having an outdoor wedding and have no plan B in case of rain? Invest in some complimentary umbrellas, and re-think having an outdoor wedding if it is not too late.

UNITY CANDLE: Some couples want to have a unity ritual in their ceremony, a metaphorical, symbolic gesture that encapsulates their relationship and the beautiful joining of their lives. Unity rituals help people understand the significance of two individuals merging their two lives into one, especially if they don't understand the language that the celebrant speaks.

Unity candles are one reason why some venues want to receive a certificate of insurance. If a couple is going to come into somebody's place and light at least three things on fire, (two taper candles, one representing each of you, and one central unity candle, representing both of you combined) they'd better be prepared to pay if they burn down the place.

Some couples choose to do a reverse unity candle. In a reverse unity candle, the couple lights their taper candles and then uses these candles to light the bridal party's candles, then they light all the guests' candles until the entire place is one gigantic fire hazard.

(See also RITUALS)

U N I T Y   R I T U A L : Unity rituals are acted-out metaphors to show that two people/families are becoming one. They're the opposite of that magic trick where the magician saws a woman in half.

(See also RITUALS)

U S H E R S : Whether guests need to be escorted to their seats formally during the ceremony or we just need them to get their asses into the chairs so we can begin the ceremony, ushers can be very useful. Ushers are folks who either pull double-duty as groomsmen or who did not make the bridal party cut but are close enough to the family that they should be involved. Ushers are like valet parking attendants, only for guests, not cars.

♥

V E N D O R S : Vendors are the exceptional men and women who make the wedding happen with their know-how and skills.

Vendors make and/or break weddings. The officiant is a vendor. The cake maker is a vendor. The ice sculpture of a nymph blowing into a horn is not a vendor, it's just an ice sculpture. The company that supplied the ice sculpture is a vendor. You are not a vendor. Or are you? I have no idea who you are.

V E N U E : The place where you hold your wedding. Ideally, it will have an indoor option because Mother Nature is unpredictable and her nicotine patch *JUST . . . ISN'T . . . WORKING.*

V E N U E   H O S T : The charismatic person assigned to be the link between what the venue can provide and what the client wants them to provide. Venue hosts are a unique combination of charmer, butler, maître d', nightclub body-guard, school principal, school janitor, and mafia soldier. If they can turn water into wine, they will. If the wine spills, they know who can clean it up. They know a guy who can get you a deal on the wine. Be kind to your venue host.

V I D E O : Many people choose to record their wedding ceremony. Indeed, people choose to record their entire wedding day.

Videographers do not just set up a still shot of your wedding ceremony like a parent capturing a grade-school play; they create heavily produced and edited montages, set to music, of the entire day, with all the moments from waking up in some hotel and remembering you are getting married to your morning spin class to having your hair done and makeup applied and dress put on and adjusted and struggling into a tux and figuring out the bow tie and losing the rings and finding the rings and traveling to the venue and forgetting the vow books in the hotel and driving back to the hotel and searching through hotel rooms and finding them and breaking speeding limits back to the venue and getting pulled over by local police and the maid of honor flirting with the cop and getting off with a warning and getting back to the venue and having a first look and the entire photo shoot and rehearsal and the glare of a disapproving future mother-in-law and the pre-ceremony jitters Jaeger shots and the actual ceremony and guests laughing doubled over then crying then leaping to their feet with ovation elation to the private post-ceremony moments and cocktail hour and reception and dinner and dances and cake and children giggling and the party and drinking and twerking and mayhem and selfies and overturned tables and clumsy passes and stolen kisses and clandestine lovemaking in coat-check rooms and the last dance and the declarations of "I love you, man" and forgetting where you parked and standing in a parking lot under a full moon thinking about the meaning of life.

So yeah, videographers charge a lot, but they are basically your Marty Scorsese for a day, so make the payment.

VOWS: Wedding vows are public declarations of intention, your spousal mission statement, and one of the most important parts of any wedding ceremony. Vows are your best shot to convince the person responsible for signing your marriage license that you are serious about what you are doing.

Vows are promises each half of a couple makes for the other. Vows are well-intended ideals expressed in terms of actionable measures. A person needs to take both a macro and micro view of the relationship's functionality in order to define and write vows.

(See also Wedding Vow Workshop, page 147)

♥

WAGNER'S BRIDAL CHORUS: One of the most recognizable pieces of wedding music throughout the world. When you hear this music, you know you're either at a wedding or you're watching a Hallmark movie with a friend who is single and who will still be single tomorrow.

This is the one that goes, "Da, DA, da-daaaaaa . . . da, *DA*, da-daaaaaaa . . ."

WEDDING: A celebration of two people who have decided to spend the rest of their lives together so they can foster a love that will make the world a better place by the power of its radiance.

An expensive way to shake down your friends for gifts.

A way to gauge how much your parents care about what other families think of them.

A rite of passage to celebrate the transition from two individual souls into one super-duper double power-soul.

An elaborate way to fool people into thinking you're straight (or gay).

An elaborate way to celebrate the love between two people, no matter their sex, gender identity, religious background, ethnicity, political leanings, or sports affiliation.

Maybe the only way we have as humans to promote love as a diplomatic solution.

W I F E : Your fiancée becomes your wife the moment you are married, which is the moment some clerk at City Hall registers your marriage a week or two after the wedding ceremony with the *thud-thwack* of an official stamp. (Or a *whirrrr* of some kind of scanning machine.)

A wife is a wonderful human being who supports you while you write a book about wedding ceremonies.

A wife holds the power in the relationship, even though she may strategically allow her husband to believe he has the power. As Toula's mother tells her in *My Big Fat Greek Wedding*, regarding the man being the head of the family: "Let me tell you something, Toula. The man may be the head, but the woman is the neck, and she can turn the head any way she wants."

A wife is a relentless husband-improver. Someone should pitch a husband-improvement show to the Oxygen Network (HIMprovement! ™©). Instead of improving a house, a wife improves her husband. We follow a couple over the course of several months, from the end of their honeymoon all the way to the day the husband, now totally improved, announces he wants a divorce.

♥

X X : Symbol for the female chromosome and the beer Dos Equis.

X Y : Symbol for the male chromosome, and sometimes the answer to a suspicious question:

"Who was that woman speaking to you at the bar, honey?"

"My X. Y?"

X X X : A Vin Diesel movie—the one where he wore a V-neck T-shirt.

♥

YO-YO MA: One of the world's finest cellists and certainly the cellist with the most fun name to say out loud. His recording of "Appalachia Waltz" (composed by Edgar Meyer, also performed with Mark O'Connor) is an achingly beautiful piece of music for a bridal entrance or any other moment in your life.

♥

ZIKA: A disease you can get from attending an outdoor wedding next to a lake in Florida.

"Did they give away any swag at the wedding?"

"No, but I caught the Zika virus from a mosquito that bit me during the ceremony and now I'm quarantined in a motel next to a mini-golf course in Sarasota."

"Was there cake?"

ACKNOWLEDGMENTS

I would never have set foot in front of a single wedding guest were it not for what I've learned from the following influencers:

My wife King Fung-Shelley has advised me on life choices for years, convincing me that I can achieve anything I put her mind to. Taj Greenlee not only introduced me to King, but he was also the one who told me I should write a book about my wedding experiences. (Mazel Taj!) Taj introduced me to Sara Kitchen, whose enthusiasm and advocacy got the idea for this book in front of the right people. Ann Treistman at The Countryman Press was the right person; she shared Sara's enthusiasm and wisely put me in the capable hands of my editor, Aurora Bell, who expertly guided this book to fruition. My agent, Lauren Abramo, has been a calm and wise influence for years, saving my writing career from myself.

At the Celebrant Foundation & Institute: Charlotte Eulette is my charismatic leader; my first celebrant teacher was Melissa Menendez and my weddings instructor was Cindy Reed. Julie Laudicina was my wedding mentor and the first to teach me about great questionnaires.

Jennifer Wright and Daniel Kibblesmith worked with me to create one of the best weddings of all time (theirs) and inspired me with their own brilliant and varied writing. Jen Spyra tutored me in the art of solid comedy-writing habits, as did Jordan Carlos and Rory Albanese. Anthony and Rebecca Russo gave me inexpressibly valuable confidence in my early days of officiating weddings. Ryan and Tatiana Brenizer hired me to marry them three times: when they eloped, when they had a big wedding, and when they threw an even bigger dance-party/musical wedding for hundreds of guests, a unique event that could be straight out of this book.

I've worked with far too many wedding planners to thank them all, but Sara Landon, Jessica Jordan, Cathy Ballone, Daniela Grafman, Amy Shey Jacobs, Donna Anello, Jeannie Uyanik, Rebecca Carrion, and Karen Brown really ought to get a shout-out here.

Fellow officiants Peter Boruchowitz and Annie Lawrence keep me sane, as do fellow celebrants Danielle Giannone, Larissa Martell, and Bettina Yiannakorou.

Rachael Ray was very generous to have me on her show.

Joan and Melissa Rivers were lovely to have me on their show.

Shayne Figueroa keeps me writing via Write Club (first rule of Write Club: no dinner until you write 1,000 words.)

Melissa Hammerle counseled me as I applied for one of the handful of spots in NYU's MFA in Fiction program. NYU also gifted me the wisdom of Brian Morton, E.L. Doctorow, and Shay Youngblood, as well as the collaborative talents of Mia Boos and Ben Rhodes.

I would not have any idea what I was doing when I perform weddings if it were not for my theater instructors. At Boston University: Jon Lipsky taught me how to make the invisible visible; Judith Chaffee taught me good posture and expression through physicality; Claudia Hill taught me accents; Bob Chapline and Rick Winter gave me vocal exercises I use to this day. From my regional theater days: my Suzuki Method instructors, Eric Hill, Will Bond, and Kate Mauer, took my shaky theatrical skills and gave them strength through stillness. Going back to the beginning, Patricia Keenan at Springfield Central High School unleashed me onto the stage, not that she had any choice.

My family members created me: my mother with limitless encouragement, good cheer, and access to the Boston Public Library; my father with a forehead-slapping way with words; my stepmother with age-defying energy; my brother with the ability to be cooler than I can ever aspire; my aunt with the quirkiest imagination.

I should also mention all of my in-laws, because part of being an in-law is being nice to your in-laws.

INDEX

K

karat, 164
Knot, The, 162, 165
knot, tying the, 166. *See also*
    handfasting

L

language, 56
live music, 34–35, 167
love story, 69–77; early days, 74; fun
    facts, 77; how did you meet?, 70;
    love, 76; obstacles, 74; proposal,
    75; readings, 77

M

maid of honor: entrance, 45; bouquet,
    89; recessional, 113; speech, 196
marriage license, 168
memory boxes, 169
music: atmosphere, 21; brides-
    maids' entrance, 42–43;
    ceremony, 34–35; groom's
    entrance, 38; groomsmen's
    entrance, 41, 43; live vs.
    canned, 34–35, 167; Pachelbel's
    "Canon in D," 32, 175; proces-
    sional, 32–34; recessional,
    112–14; Wagner's Bridal Cho-
    rus, 199; Yo-Yo Ma, 201

O

objections, 172
obstacles, 74
officiant, 172
officiant, notes for, 15, 56, 69, 79
open bar, 174
outdoor weddings, 173

P

Pachelbel's "Canon in D," 32, 175
parents: entrance, 37, 39, 47; thanks,
    59–60
performance: accents, 82; enunciate, 80; images, 79; rehearse,
    80; senses, 82; speaking up, 79;
    vary the pacing, 80–81; voices,
    81–82; writing to voice, 80
permission from parents, 180–81
pets, 175–76
photo shoot, 177
photographers, 176
Pinterest, 178
presentation of the couple, 110
processional: music, 32–35;
    no-cessional, 51–52. *See also*
    entrances
pronouncement of marriage,
    109–10
proposal, 75, 180

Q

questionnaire, 183
questions for couples, 139–45

R

readings, 77, 82–84, 184
recessional, 112–14, 188
registry, 188
rehearsal, 189
rehearsal dinner, 189
religious traditions, 100
ring bear, 45, 189
ring bearers: blended families, 47;
    entrance, 45–46; recessional,
    113. See also ring bear
ring exchange, 97–98
ring warming, 189
rings, 190
rings, during ceremony, 98–99
rituals, 99–101, 191
RSVP, 191
runner, 191

S

same-sex wedding, 192; "First
    Look," 36; parental permission,

Christopher Shelley has been officiating weddings since 2011. He has a BFA in Acting from Boston University and an MFA in Creative Writing from New York University. After becoming a certified Life-Cycle Celebrant through the Celebrant Foundation & Institute, he's performed weddings in settings as diverse as the New York Public Library, The Park Plaza Hotel, The Roosevelt Hotel, The Brooks Atkinson Theater (Broadway!), Citi Field (where the Mets try), Grand Central Station, all over Central Park, on dinner boats and rooftops, in wineries, repurposed warehouses, breweries, mansions, country clubs, hotel suites, and one old retired cop's living room in Brooklyn. He has appeared on *The Rachael Ray Show* to officiate weddings several times and hosted a memorial service for Joan Rivers' dog on the late comedienne's show, *Joan & Melissa: Joan Knows Best*. He has published short fiction in several online magazines and his story "Tongue Tricks" was nominated for a 2008 Pushcart Prize—it didn't win; he just likes the anecdote. Chris writes and performs wedding ceremonies through his company Illuminating Ceremonies, where he also writes reception speeches for best men and maids of honor. He lives in New York and Cincinnati with his smart wife, King.